Contents

Traditional Peanut Butter 5

Sugar Pie 5

Cheese Frosting 6

Ritz Stew 7

Cinnamon Pumpkin Loaves 7

Crunchy Amish Coleslaw With Nutmeg 9

Friendship Pancakes 10

Creamy Potato And Bread Casserole 11

Fried Tunnel Cakes 12

Green Stew Pan 13

Creamy Cheese Spread 14

Maraschino Pudding 15

Amish Potato Salad From Cook's Country 17

Brown Oats Cheesecake 18

Warm Tart Apple Salad 20

Cinnamon Muffins 22

Friendship Cake 23

Confectioner Vanilla Galletes 24

Hamish Burgers 26

Warm Lima Salad 27

Herbed Chicken Stuffing 28

Creamy Velveeta Bake 29

Apple Pie Brownies 31

Fairies Cake 32

Roasted Pasta Stew 33

Tropical Jell-O Salad 34

Cheesy Potato Casserole 35

Coconut Pudding.. 36

Sweet Mustard Dressing 37

Hen Tart 38

Beef Borcht 39

Scalloped Potato.. 41

Festive Buttermilk Bread 42

Hash Brown Loaf... 43

Creamy Corn Casserole 44

Caramel Delight 45

Juicy Apple Pies.. 46

Cinnamon Cookies... 47

Rolled Walnuts Tart... 48

Allspice Tart.. 49

Glazed Crisco Puffs 51

Valentine Strawberry Amish Bread 52

Spicy Orange Bread 53

Poppy Bread... 54

Splenda Muffins.. 56

Nutty Carrot Muffins 57

Juniper Stir Fry 58

Hot Cornmeal 59

Slow Burger Stew 60

Creamy Jell-O And Egg Salad 60

Chicken Farm Soup 61

Creamy Chicken Roast 62

Applesauce Muffins 63

Vanilla Coffee Cake 64

Banana Cake With Vanilla Frosting 65

Vanilla Blondies 67

Amish Mint Tea 68

Crunchy Broccoli With Cheddar Sauce 69

Condensed Maple Tart 70

Salisbury Steak With Mushroom Sauce 71

Quick Corn And Egg Soup 72

Sweet Spicy Raisins Sauce 73

Rhubarb Rolls With Vanilla Sauce 74

Caramen Pecan Cake 76

Starter Amish Biscuits 77

Endive Salad With Bacon Dressing 79

Homemade Ketchup 80

Classic Cheese Corn 81

Peanut Crackers 82

Sweet And Salty Beef Chili 83

Tropical Marshmallow Delight 84

Cheesy Beef And Noodles Casserole 85

Easy Amish Friendship Starter 86

Alternative 2-Ingredient Amish Starter 87

Sunny Cornbread 88

Creamy Noodles And Beef Casserole.. 89

Homemade Amish Noodles 90

Whipped Lemon Tart.. 91

Crisco And Buttermilk Cookies.. 92

Tartar Tart.. 93

2 9-Inch Pie Shells, Unbaked.. 94

TRADITIONAL PEANUT BUTTER

INGREDIENTS

- 1/2 C. creamy **peanut butter** 1/4 C. **marshmallow** crème

- 1 C. light **corn syrup**

DIRECTIONS

- Get a large mixing bowl: Combine in it all the ingredients and beat them until they become smooth.

- Transfer the mix to a container and place it in the fridge until ready to serve.

- Enjoy.

SERVINGS: 1

Preparation 10 mins- -**Total Time** 10 mins

NUTRITIONAL INFORMATION:

Calories 1270.7, Fat 43.9g, Cholesterol 0.0mg, Sodium 565.9mg, Carbohydrates 221.2g, Protein 1.8g

SUGAR PIE

INGREDIENTS

- 1/3 C. **butter**

- 1 1/2 C. brown **sugar**

- 2 **eggs**

- 1 tbsp all-purpose **flour**

- 1/2 C. evaporated **milk**

- 1 9" unbaked **pie shell**

DIRECTIONS

- Before you do anything, preheat the oven to 350 F. Grease a pie pan and place it aside.

- Get a large mixing bowl: Cream in it the butter, brown sugar, eggs, flour, and milk.

- Place the shell in the pan and pour the filling into it. Place it in the oven and let it cook for 16 min.

- Allow it to cool down completely for 1 h in the oven then serve it with your favorite toppings.

- Enjoy.

SERVINGS: 1

Preparation 15 mins

NUTRITIONAL INFORMATION:

Calories 2656.2, Fat 115.4g, Cholesterol 622.0mg, Sodium 1379.8mg, Carbohydrates 387.8g, Protein 28.9g

CHEESE FROSTING

INGREDIENTS

- 8 oz. cream **cheese**

- 2/3 C. brown **sugar**

- 1 tsp **vanilla**

- 1/8 tsp **salt**

- 2 C. **Cool Whip**

DIRECTIONS

- Get a large mixing bowl: Cream in it the cream cheese, sugar, vanilla and salt until they become light and smooth.

- Stir in the cool whip. Place the frosting in the fridge until ready to use.

- Enjoy.

SERVINGS: 1

Preparation 5 mins- -**Total Time** 5 mins

NUTRITIONAL INFORMATION:

Calories 1826.2, Fat 115.7g, Cholesterol 249.9mg, Sodium 1099.1mg, Carbohydrates 188.9g, Protein 15.5g

RITZ STEW

INGREDIENTS

- 2 tbsp **butter**

- 2 C. **milk**

- 1 (4 oz.) packet **Ritz**

DIRECTIONS

- Place a heavy saucepan over medium heat. Stir in the butter until it melts and become slightly brown.

- Stir in the milk and heat it through.

- Get a large mixing bowl: Place in it the crackers. Pour the milk mix all over them and let sit for a while.

- Serve your ritz for breakfast.

- Enjoy.

SERVINGS: 4

Preparation 5 mins- -**Total Time** 15 mins

NUTRITIONAL INFORMATION:

Calories 268.4, Fat 16.8g, Cholesterol 32.3mg, Sodium 360.5mg, Carbohydrates 23.6g, Protein 6.1g

CINNAMON PUMPKIN LOAVES

INGREDIENTS

- 3 C. **sugar**

- 1 C. vegetable **oil**

- 4 **eggs**, beaten

- 1 (1 lb) can **pumpkin**

- 3 1/2 C. **flour**

- 2 tsp **baking soda**

- 2 tsp **salt**

- 1/2 tsp **clove**

- 1 tsp **cinnamon**

- 1 tsp **allspice**

- 1 tsp **nutmeg**

- 2/3 C. **water**

- 1 C. chopped **nuts**

DIRECTIONS

- Before you do anything, preheat the oven to 350 F. Grease 4

- bread pans and place them aside.

- Get a large mixing bowl: Beat in it the sugar, oil and eggs.

- Mix in the pumpkin followed by the flour, baking soda salt, clove, cinnamon, allspice, nutmeg and water at last.

- Fold the nuts into the batter and pour it into the pans. Place them in the oven and let them cook for 60 min.

- Allow bread loaves to cool down completely then serve them.

- Enjoy.

SERVINGS: 1

Preparation 15 mins

NUTRITIONAL INFORMATION:

Calories 3140.3, Fat 121.9g, Cholesterol 423.0mg, Sodium 3734.8mg, Carbohydrates 484.9g,Protein 37.6g

CRUNCHY AMISH COLESLAW WITH NUTMEG

DRESSING

INGREDIENTS

- DRESSING

- 2 large **eggs**

- 3 tbsp granulated **sugar**

- 1 1/2 tbsp all-purpose **flour**

- 1 1/4 tsp **salt**

- 1/2 tsp ground **mustard**

- 1/4 C. cider **vinegar**

- 1/4 C. **water**

- 1 tbsp **butter**

- 3 tbsp **cream**

- COLESLAW

- 6 C. shredded **cabbage**

- 1 large shredded **carrot**

- 1 **celery**, chopped

- 1 small **onion**, chopped

- 1/2 green bell **pepper**, chopped 1/4 C. minced **parsley**

- 1 1/2 tsp **celery** seeds

- 1 tsp **mustard** seeds

- 1/2 tsp coarse ground black **pepper**

DIRECTIONS

- Get a heavy saucepan. Whisk in it the eggs then add to them the sugar, flour, salt and mustard gradually while mixing all the time.

- Mix in the vinegar and the water followed by oil and butter until you get a smooth mix.

- Let the dressing cook over low heat for 7 min while stirring it all

- the time until they become creamy.

- Add to them the cream and whisk them well. Place it aside to cool down completely.

- Get a large mixing bowl: Stir in it all the veggies with mustard seeds, salt and pepper.

- Drizzle the dressing over them and toss them to coat. Place the salad in the fridge until ready to serve.

- Enjoy.

SERVINGS: 5

Preparation 10 mins- -**Total Time** 15 mins

NUTRITIONAL INFORMATION:

Calories 160.0, Fat 7.7g, Cholesterol 100.7mg, Sodium 664.6mg, Carbohydrates 19.0g, Protein 5.0g

FRIENDSHIP PANCAKES

INGREDIENTS

- 1 **egg**

- 1 C. Amish **starter,** see appendix 1/2 C. **milk**

- 2 tbsp **oil**

- 1 tsp **vanilla**

- 1 1/2 tsp **baking powder**

- 1 C. **flour**

DIRECTIONS

- Get a large mixing bowl: Cream in it the egg with Amish starter, milk, oil and vanilla.

- Beat in it the flour with baking powder. Mix in a splash of milk if the batter is too thick.

- Place a griddle over medium heat. Grease it with a cooking spray.

- Spread in it 1/4 C. of the pancake batter.

- Let it cook until it becomes golden brown on each side. Repeat the process with the remaining batter.

- Serve your pancakes with your favorite toppings.

- Enjoy.

SERVINGS: 4

Preparation 5 mins- -**Total Time** 25 mins

NUTRITIONAL INFORMATION:

Calories 215.1, Fat 9.4g, Cholesterol 50.7mg, Sodium 169.5mg, Carbohydrates 25.9g, Protein 5.8g

CREAMY POTATO AND BREAD CASSEROLE

INGREDIENTS

- 1 1/2 C. **turnips,** grated

- 1 1/2 C. **potatoes**, grated

- 3/4 C. **milk**

- 1/2 C. plain **yogurt**

- 1/2 C. whole wheat **bread** crumbs 1/4 C. vegetable **oil**

- 2 medium **onions**, chopped

- 1 tbsp dried **parsley**

- 1/2 tsp **pepper**

salt

DIRECTIONS

- Before you do anything, preheat the oven to 375 F. Grease casserole dish and place it aside.

- Get a large mixing bowl: Combine in it the turnips with potato, milk, yogurt, oil, onion, parsley, pepper and salt.

- Pour the mix into the casserole dish. Top it with the breadcrumbs.

- Place the casserole in the oven and let it cook for 42 min. Serve it hot.

- Enjoy.

SERVINGS: 6

Preparation 10 mins- -**Total Time** 50 mins

NUTRITIONAL INFORMATION:

Calories 213.1, Fat 11.7g, Cholesterol 6.9mg, Sodium 150.1mg, Carbohydrates 23.6g, Protein 5.0g

FRIED TUNNEL CAKES

INGREDIENTS

- 3 -4 C. **flour**

- 3 **eggs**

- 2 C. **milk**

- 1/4 C. **sugar**

- 2 tsp **baking powder**

- 1/2 tsp **salt**

- powdered **sugar** oil

DIRECTIONS

- Before you do anything, preheat the oven to 350 F.

- Get a large mixing bowl: Cream in it the egg with milk and sugar.

- Get a mixing bowl: Stir in it the flour with baking powder and salt. Add it to the eggs mix and combine them well.

- Pour 1 C. of the butter in a funnel with an half inch opening.

- Place a heavy pan over medium heat and heat in it about 1/8 inch of oil.

- Squeeze the funnel to get the batter out into the hot oil drizzling it in circular and messy motion until you get a 6 to 8 inches cake.

- Cook the cake in the hot oil until it become golden brown on each side.

- Repeat the process with the remaining ingredients. Serve your golden cakes with your favorite toppings.

- Enjoy.

SERVINGS: 6

Preparation 10 mins- -**Total Time** 15 mins

NUTRITIONAL INFORMATION:

Calories 349.3, Fat 6.0g, Cholesterol 117.1mg, Sodium 390.9mg, Carbohydrates 60.3g, Protein 12.2g

GREEN STEW PAN

INGREDIENTS

- 6 slices turkey bacon

- 3 medium onions, sliced

- 1 lb fresh green beans, cleaned and cut into small pieces 2 C. fresh diced tomatoes

- 1 tsp salt

- 1/2 tsp pepper

- 1/3 C. boiling water

DIRECTIONS

- Place a large pan over medium heat. Cook in it the bacon until it become crisp.

- Stir in the onion and let it cook for 10 min while stirring it often.

- Add the green beans and cook them for 4 min.

- Stir in the tomato with water, salt and pepper. Lower the heat and let them cook for 10 min until the veggies are done. Serve it warm.

- Get a large mixing bowl:

- Allow it to cool down completely then serve it with your favorite toppings.

- Enjoy.

SERVINGS: 6

Preparation 20 mins- -**Total Time** 50 mins

NUTRITIONAL INFORMATION:

Calories 173.4, Fat 10.4g, Cholesterol 15.4mg, Sodium 771.7mg, Carbohydrates 16.7g, Protein 5.2g

CREAMY CHEESE SPREAD

INGREDIENTS

- 3 1/2 C. water

- 4 C. milk

- 2 1/2 tsp baking soda

- 5 lbs white processed cheese or 5 lbs yellow American cheese Directions

- Place a heavy saucepan over medium heat: Heat in it the milk with water until they start boiling.

- Stir in the cheese with baking soda until they melt. Use a hand whisk to whisk them until they become creamy.

- Serve your spread with some bread or over a salad.

- Enjoy.

SERVINGS: 1

Preparation 15 mins- -**Total Time** 25 mins

NUTRITIONAL INFORMATION:

Calories 4054.5, Fat 303.4g, Cholesterol 975.5mg, Sodium 16165.7mg, Carbohydrates 111.4g, Protein 224.6g

MARASCHINO PUDDING

INGREDIENTS

- 6 oz. orange **gelatin**

- 3 oz. lemon **gelatin**

- 10 oz. chunk **pineapple**, drained 10 oz. miniature **marshmallows**

- 8 oz. **Cool Whip**

- 6 oz. maraschino **cherries**, drained Directions

- Get a large mixing bowl: Prepare in it the orange gelatin by following the instructions on the package.

- Get another mixing bowl: Prepare in it the lemon gelatin by following the instructions on the package.

- Place both of them in the fridge until they harden.

- Remove the cherries with pineapple from their liquid. Stir them in a serving bowl with the lemon and orange gelatin.

- Place the pudding in the fridge for 4 h at least then serve it.

- Enjoy.

SERVINGS: 4

Preparation 2 hrs

NUTRITIONAL INFORMATION:

Calories 779.6, Fat 14.6g, Cholesterol 0.0mg, Sodium 370.9mg, Carbohydrates 161.9g, Protein 7.3g

FALL TART

INGREDIENTS

- 1 C. **pumpkin**

- 1 C. brown **sugar**

- 1/2 C. granulated **sugar**

- 1/2 C. **molasses**

- 2 **egg** yolks, beaten

- 2 **egg** whites, beaten until stiff 2 tbsp **flour**

- 2 C. scalded **milk**

- pumpkin pie **spice**

DIRECTIONS

- Before you do anything, preheat the oven to 400 F. Grease a baking pan and place it aside.

- Get a large mixing bowl: Stir in it the flour with sugars.

- Get a large mixing bowl: Beat in it the pumpkin, yolks & molasses until they become smooth. Mix in the milk with browned butter, spices.

- Mix in it the flour mix. Pour the filling into a pie shell. Place it in the oven and let it cook for 12 min.

- Lower the temperature to 350 F. Let the tart cook for an extra 42 min. Allow it to cool down completely then serve it with your favorite toppings. Enjoy.

SERVINGS: 1

Preparation 15 mins- -**Total Time** 55 mins

NUTRITIONAL INFORMATION:

Calories 1118.6, Fat 13.2g, Cholesterol 222.9mg, Sodium 256.4mg, Carbohydrates 241.8g, Protein 15.4g

AMISH POTATO SALAD FROM COOK'S COUNTRY

INGREDIENTS

- 3 lbs Yukon gold **potatoes**, peeled and cut into chunks **salt** and **pepper**

- 1/3 C. cider **vinegar**

- 1/4 C. **sugar**

- 2 tbsp yellow **mustard**

- 4 large hard-cooked **eggs**, peeled 1/2 tsp **celery** seed

- 3/4 C. sour **cream**

- 1 **celery** rib, chopped

DIRECTIONS

- Place a large pot of water over high. Stir in 1 tbsp of salt and bring it to a boil.

- Add to it the potatoes and let them cook for 12 min over medium heat.

- Get a microwave safe bowl: Stir in it the sugar with vinegar.

- Place it in the microwave for 32 min.

- Get a blender: Combine in it the vinegar mix with mustard, 1

- hard-cooked egg yolk , celery seed, and ½ tsp salt. Blend them smooth to make the dressing.

- Get a large mixing bowl: Drain the potatoes and stir them into it with 2 tbsp of the dressing.

- Place it in the fridge for 35 min.

- Get a mixing bowl: Combine in it the remaining dressing with sour cream. Stir into them the remaining eggs and mash them.

- Stir in the chilled potato with celery. Adjust the seasoning of the salad then place it in the fridge for 32 min. Serve it.

- Enjoy.

SERVINGS: 8

Preparation 1 hr

NUTRITIONAL INFORMATION:

Calories 261.3, Fat 7.4g, Cholesterol 115.4mg, Sodium 67.8mg, Carbohydrates 42.1g, Protein 7.1g

BROWN OATS CHEESECAKE

INGREDIENTS

- CRUST

- 1/2 C. **butter**, melted

- 1/4 C. packed brown **sugar**

- 1 C. whole wheat **flour**

- 1 C. regular rolled **oats**

- 1/4 tsp ground **cinnamon**

- FILLING

- 16 oz. cream **cheese**

- 1 1/4 C. dairy **buttermilk**

- 2 large **eggs**

- 1/4 C. brown **sugar**

- 1 tbsp all-purpose **flour**

- 1 tsp **baking soda**

- 1 tsp **vanilla**

- TOPPING

- 3/4 C. soft coconut **macaroon**, crushed

DIRECTIONS

- Before you do anything, preheat the oven to 350 F. Line up a spring form and place it aside.

- Mix the melted butter with brown sugar, flour and oats well. Press the mix into the pan and place it aside.

- Get a large mixing bowl: Cream in it the brown sugar with cream cheese until they become creamy.

- Mix in the buttermilk, flour and soda followed by the eggs and vanilla until you a creamy mix to make the filling.

- Pour the filling over the crust and lay over it the macarons. Place

- the cheesecake in the oven and let it cook for 1 h 12 min.

- Allow the cake to cool down completely. Serve it with your favorite toppings.

- Enjoy.

SERVINGS: 12

Preparation 15 mins

NUTRITIONAL INFORMATION:

Calories 319.9, Fat 22.5g, Cholesterol 98.1mg, Sodium 314.1mg, Carbohydrates 23.5g, Protein 7.3g

WARM TART APPLE SALAD

INGREDIENTS

- 1/4 lb **turkey bacon**, diced

- 1/2 C. chopped **onion**

- 2 medium tart **apples**, peeled and chopped 5 C. shredded red **cabbage**

- 1/4 C. cider **vinegar**, plus

- 2 tbsp cider **vinegar**

- 1/4 C. brown **sugar**, plus

- 2 tbsp brown **sugar**

- 1/2 tsp ground **allspice**

- 1/4 tsp **salt**

- 1/4 tsp black **pepper**

DIRECTIONS

- Place a large saucepan over medium heat: Stir in it the bacon, onion, and apples. let them cook for 4 min.

- Stir in the cabbage and cook them for an extra 11 min. Stir in the rest of the ingredients.

- Lower the heat and put on the lid then cook them for 22 min.

- Once the time is up, serve your salad warm.

- Enjoy.

SERVINGS: 6

Preparation 15 mins- -**Total Time** 35 mins

NUTRITIONAL INFORMATION:

Calories 189.9, Fat 8.7g, Cholesterol 12.8mg, Sodium 277.3mg, Carbohydrates 25.8g, Protein 3.2g

SPICY APPLE CRISP

INGREDIENTS

- 9 **apples**, peeled and sliced

- 1 C. **flour**

- 1 tsp **baking powder**

- 1 pinch **salt**

- 1 large **egg**

- 4 tbsp **butter**, melted

- 1 tsp **cinnamon**

- 1 tsp **cardamom**

DIRECTIONS

- Before you do anything, preheat the oven to 350 F. Grease a baking pan and place it aside.

- Get a large mixing bowl: Stir in it the flour, sugar, baking powder and salt.

- Add to them the egg and mix them well.

- Place the apple slices in the baking pan. Spread the flour mix over it. Drizzle the melted butter on top followed by the cinnamon and cardamom.

- Place the pan in the oven and let cook for 35 to 40 min. Serve it with some ice cream.

- Enjoy.

SERVINGS: 4

Preparation 20 mins

NUTRITIONAL INFORMATION:

Calories 399.0, Fat 13.6g, Cholesterol 83.4mg, Sodium 232.7mg, Carbohydrates 67.9g, Protein 5.8g

CINNAMON MUFFINS

INGREDIENTS

- MUFFINS

- 1 1/2 C. unbleached all-purpose **flour** 1 1/2 tsp **baking powder**

- 1/2 tsp **salt**

- 1/4 tsp **mace**

- 1/2 C. **sugar**

- 1/3 C. canola **oil**

- 1 **egg**

- 1 tsp **vanilla**

- 1/2 C. **milk**

- COATING

- 6 tbsp **butter**, melted

- 1/2 C. **sugar**

- 1 tsp **cinnamon**

DIRECTIONS

- Before you do anything, preheat the oven to 350 F. Grease a muffins pan and place it aside.

- Get a large mixing bowl: Stir in it the flour, baking powder, salt and mace.

- Get a large mixing bowl: Cream in it the sugar, oil, egg and vanilla. Mix in the flour and milk gradually.

- Pour the batter into 10 muffins C.. Place them in the oven and let them cook for 18 to 22 min.

- Get a mixing bowl: Stir in it 1/2 C. sugar and the cinnamon.

- Dip the muffins in the melted butter while they are hot then roll them in the sugar mix.

- Serve them warm.

- Enjoy.

SERVINGS: 10

Preparation 20 mins- -**Total Time** 40 mins

NUTRITIONAL INFORMATION:

Calories 288.4, Fat 15.3g, Cholesterol 41.1mg, Sodium 233.2mg, Carbohydrates 35.3g, Protein 3.0g

FRIENDSHIP CAKE

INGREDIENTS

- CAKE

- 1 C. room temp. **butter**

- 1 C. granulated **sugar**

- 1 C. dark brown **sugar**

- 2 tsp **vanilla** extract

- 3 C. all-purpose **flour**

- 1 1/2 tsp **salt**

- 2 C. dairy **buttermilk**

- TOPPING

- 7 tbsp **butter**, melted

- 1 C. dark brown **sugar**

- 1/4 tsp grated fresh **nutmeg**

- 1/4 C. whole **milk**

- 1/2 C. chopped **pecans**

DIRECTIONS

- Before you do anything, preheat the oven to 350 F. Grease a cake pan and place it aside.

- Get a large mixing bowl: Beat in it the sugars with butter for 4 min.

- Get a mixing bowl: Stir in the flour with salt. Mix them into the butter cream with buttermilk gradually.

- Transfer the batter into the cake pan. Cook them in the oven for 32 to 35 min.

- Get a mixing bowl: Mix in it the melted butter with brown sugar, nutmeg, milk and nuts to make the topping.

- Sprinkle the toppings over the cake and cook it in the oven for 3 min. Serve it after it completely cools down.

- Enjoy.

SERVINGS: 12

Preparation 10 mins- -**Total Time** 50 mins

NUTRITIONAL INFORMATION:

Calories 564.5, Fat 26.1g, Cholesterol 60.6mg, Sodium 507.2mg, Carbohydrates 79.1g, Protein 5.3g

CONFECTIONER VANILLA GALLETES

INGREDIENTS

- 3 large **eggs**

- 2 tsp **vanilla** extract

- 2 tsp **salt**

- 1 C. heavy whipping **cream**

- 4 C. unbleached all-purpose **flour** 2 liters vegetable **oil**

- 1 C. confectioners powdered icing **sugar** 1/2 tsp ground **cinnamon**

DIRECTIONS

- Before you do anything, preheat the oven to 425 F. Grease a loaf pan and place it aside.

- Get a large mixing bowl: Cream n it the eggs until they become frothy.

- Mix in the vanilla, salt, and the cream. Mix in the flour gradually until you get a smooth dough.

- Transfer the dough to a lightly floured surface and knead it for several minutes until it becomes soft.

- Place a deep pan over high heat and heat in it 1/4 inch of oil.

- Divide the dough into 8 portions. Roll each one into a thin circle.

- Place a dough circle in the hot oil and cook it for 2 to 3 min on each side until it become golden brown.

- Drain it and repeat the process with the remaining dough.

- Sprinkle some icing sugar and cinnamon over the galletes then serve them.

- Enjoy.

SERVINGS: 1

Preparation 50 mins- -**Total Time** 1 hr

NUTRITIONAL INFORMATION:

Calories 410.1, Fat 40.7g, Cholesterol 20.0mg, Sodium 103.4mg, Carbohydrates 10.6g , Protein 1.5g

HAMISH BURGERS

INGREDIENTS

- 1 head **lettuce**, shredded

- 4 **tomatoes**, diced

- 1 large **onion**, diced

- 1 (14 oz.) bags tortilla **chips**, crushed 3 lbs ground **beef**

- 1 C. hard-boiled **egg**, diced

- 1 lb saltine **crackers**, crushed 2 C. cooked **rice**

- 4 (10 3/4 oz.) cans cheddar **cheese** soup 1 C. diced **pecans**

- 1 (16 oz.) cartons sour **cream**

- 1 C. chopped **carrot**

- 1 C. diced green **pepper**

- 1 C. **sunflower** seeds

- 1 (10 oz.) jars **salsa**

DIRECTIONS

- Lay tortilla chips on serving plates and top it with rice.

- Place a large skillet over medium heat. Cook in it the beef for 20

- min until it is perfectly brown.

- Drain it and stir it into it the tomato sauce with sour cream and cheddar soup. Cook them for an extra 10 min.

- Spoon the beef mixture over the rice layer followed by the veggies, eggs, sunflower seeds, pecans, and crackers. Serve them right away.

- Enjoy.

SERVINGS: 15

Preparation 15 mins- -**Total Time** 25 mins

NUTRITIONAL INFORMATION:

Calories 776.0, Fat 46.1g, Cholesterol 130.7mg, Sodium 1228.9mg, Carbohydrates 61.3g, Protein 31.2g

WARM LIMA SALAD

INGREDIENTS

- 1 lb lima **beans**

- 4 **potatoes**, diced

- 2 oz. **turkey**, cubed

- 1 1/4 C. half-and-half **cream**

- 1 tbsp **butter**

- 1/4 C. chopped **parsley**

- 1 tsp grated **nutmeg**

DIRECTIONS

- Place a large pot over medium heat. Stir in it the potato with beans. Pour over them enough water to cover them.

- Cook them until they start boiling. Lower the heat and let them cook for 22 min.

- Discard the water. Stir the turkey, half and half, butter, parsley and nutmeg into the pot. Season them with some salt and pepper.

- Serve your salad warm.

- Enjoy.

SERVINGS: 4

Preparation 5 mins- -**Total Time** 30 mins

HERBED CHICKEN STUFFING

INGREDIENTS

- 2 lbs white **bread**, cut in cubes 2 lbs **chicken** thighs, Poached 1/2 C. **parsley**, Minced

- 3/4 C. **onion**, Chopped

- 1 C. **celery**, Chopped

- 1 C. **carrot**, Shredded

- 1 1/4 C. **potatoes**, boiled, chopped 1 tbsp rubbed **sage**

- 1 tbsp **celery** seed

- 1 tsp dried **thyme**

- 1/2 tsp black **pepper**

- 1/2 tbsp **turmeric**

- 5 **eggs**

- 12 oz. evaporated **milk**

- 2 1/2 C. homemade chicken **broth**

DIRECTIONS

- Before you do anything, preheat the oven to 350 F. Grease a casserole dish and place it aside.

- Spread the bread cubes on 2 baking sheets. Place them in the oven and bake them for 16 min.

- In the meantime, discard the chicken bones and skin then shred the meat.

- Get a large mixing bowl: Stir in it the toasted bread with the shredded chicken, chopped veggies and seasonings.

- Get another mixing bowl: Whisk in it the eggs with broth and milk. Add them to the bread mix and combine them well.

- Cover the bowl and let it sit for 1 h. Once the time is up, pour it into the casserole dish.

- Place the pan in the oven and let it cook for 1 h. Serve it warm.

- Enjoy.

SERVINGS: 20

Preparation 0 mins- -**Total Time** 0 mins

NUTRITIONAL INFORMATION:

Calories 306.6, Fat 11.5g, Cholesterol 89.8mg, Sodium 465.0mg, Carbohydrates 33.7g, Protein 16.0g

CREAMY VELVEETA BAKE

INGREDIENTS

- 1 C. **Spam**, diced

- 1 C. elbow **macaroni**

- 1/2 lb Velveeta **cheese**

- 1 C. unseasoned **breadcrumbs**

- 2 C. frozen **peas**

- 3 tbsp **flour**

- 3 tbsp **butter**

- 2 C. **milk**

- 1/2 tsp **salt**

- 1/2 tsp **pepper**

DIRECTIONS

- Before you do anything, preheat the oven to 425 F. Grease a casserole dish and place it aside.

- Prepare the macaroni according to the directions on the package cooking for half of the recommended time only.

- Place a heavy saucepan over medium heat: Stir in it the four with butter. Add to them the milk while mixing all the time.

- Stir into it half of the Velveeta cheese until it completely melts to make the white sauce.

- Stir the spam with cooked macaroni and the white sauce in the casserole dish. Place it in the oven and let it cook for 46 min.

- Serve it hot.

- Enjoy.

SERVINGS: 4

Preparation 15 mins- -**Total Time** 1 hr

NUTRITIONAL INFORMATION:

Calories 696.7, Fat 41.7g, Cholesterol 123.9mg, Sodium 2158.6mg, Carbohydrates 51.3g, Protein 29.1g

CRUNCHY BEET SALAD

INGREDIENTS

- 1 cooked **beet**, sliced

- 4 heads curly endive **lettuce**, washed, sliced 2 tsp **parsley**, chopped

- 2 tsp **tarragon**, chopped

- 2 tsp **chervil**, chopped

- 1/4 tsp **salt**

- 1/8 tsp black **pepper**, ground 3 tbsp olive **oil**

- 1 1/2 tbsp apple cider **vinegar**

DIRECTIONS

- Get a serving bowl: Lay in it the lettuce then top it with the beets, sprinkle with parsley, tarragon, and chervil.

- Add to them the olive oil with vinegar, a pinch of salt and pepper.

- Mix them well. Serve your salad right away.

- Enjoy.

SERVINGS: 4

Preparation 30 mins- -**Total Time** 30 mins

NUTRITIONAL INFORMATION:

Calories 185.9, Fat 11.2g, Cholesterol 0.0mg, Sodium 269.2mg, Carbohydrates 19.1g, Protein 6.9g

APPLE PIE BROWNIES

INGREDIENTS

- 1 C. **butter**, softened

- 1 3/4 C. **sugar**

- 2 **eggs**, well beaten

- 1 tsp **vanilla**

- 2 C. **flour**

- 1 tsp **baking powder**

- 1 tsp **baking soda**

- 1 tsp cinnamon

- 1/2 tsp **salt**

- 2 C. baking **apples**, peeled and chopped 1/2 C. **walnuts**

DIRECTIONS

- Before you do anything, preheat the oven to 350 F. Grease a baking pan and place it aside.

- Get a large mixing bowl: Beat in it the butter, sugar, eggs and vanilla until they become slight and smooth.

- Mix into it the flour with baking powder, baking soda, cinnamon, and salt.

- Fold the walnuts with apples into the batter. Pour it into the greased pan. Cook the brownies in the oven for 46 min.

- Allow the brownie pan to cool down completely then cut into squares and serve it.

- Enjoy.

SERVINGS: 9

Preparation 20 mins- -**Total Time** 1 hr 5 mins

NUTRITIONAL INFORMATION:

Calories 508.0, Fat 26.1g, Cholesterol 101.2mg, Sodium 471.2mg, Carbohydrates 65.2g , Protein 5.5g

FAIRIES CAKE

INGREDIENTS

- 10 **eggs**

- 1/2 tsp cream of **tartar**

- 1 dash **salt**

- 1 tbsp **water**

- 3/4 C. cake **flour**

- 1 C. **sugar**

- 1 tsp **vanilla**

DIRECTIONS

- Before you do anything, preheat the oven to 350 F. Grease a cake pan and place it aside.

- Get a large mixing bowl: Mix in it the egg whites with a hand mixer until they become light.

- Mix in it the cream of tartar and beat them until their soft peaks.

- Get a mixing bowl: Cream in it the egg yolks and salt. Mix in the water gradually followed by the sugar until its soft peaks.

- Stir the flour with egg whites into the egg yolk batter. Pour it into the cake pan and cook it for 42 min in the oven.

- Allow it to cool down completely then serve it with your favorite toppings.

- Enjoy.

SERVINGS: 10

Preparation 25 mins- -**Total Time** 1 hr 5 mins

NUTRITIONAL INFORMATION:

Calories 189.6, Fat 5.0g, Cholesterol 211.5mg, Sodium 85.8mg, Carbohydrates 28.5g, Protein 7.1g

ROASTED PASTA STEW

INGREDIENTS

- 1/4 C. beef **bouillon** granules 10 C. hot **water**

- 3 lbs boneless **chuck** roast, trimmed 8 whole **cloves**

- 3 **celery** ribs, chopped

- 2 large **carrots**, peeled, chopped 1 large **onion**, quartered

- 1 seeded green bell **pepper**, quartered 1 bunch **parsley** sprig, plus

- 1/2 C. **parsley**, chopped

- 2 **bay** leaves

- 1/2 tsp ground **pepper**

- 1 (16 oz.) packages egg **noodles**

- 1 tsp **salt**

- freshly-ground **pepper**

DIRECTIONS

- Before you do anything, preheat the oven to 350 F. Grease a casserole dish and place it aside.

- Get a large oven proof pot. Stir in it the beef bouillon with water.

- Stir into them the chuck roast, cloves, celery, carrots, onion, green pepper and parsley sprigs.

- Put on the lid and place the pot in the oven. Let it cook for 3 h 10 min.

- Drain the roast and shred it. Drain the veggies and finely chop them. Stir them back into the pot with the shredded roast.

- add the noodles with a pinch of salt and pepper. Put on the lid and place the pot in the oven. Let it cook for 35 min.

- Serve your stew hot warm.

- Enjoy.

SERVINGS: 12

Preparation

NUTRITIONAL INFORMATION:

Calories 450.1, Fat 23.9g, Cholesterol 110.1mg, Sodium 319.3mg, Carbohydrates 30.5g, Protein 26.7g

TROPICAL JELL-O SALAD

INGREDIENTS

- 1 (3 oz.) packet orange **Jell-O**

- 1 tsp **sugar**

- 1 C. boiling **water**

- 1 C. cold **water**

- 1/2 C. **carrot**, peeled and shredded 1/2 C. canned crushed **pineapple**, drained

DIRECTIONS

- Get a casserole dish: Stir in it the Jell-O with sugar and boiling water. Whisk them for 3 min.

- Add the cold water to the mix. Place the dish in the fridge and let it sit for 42 min.

- Lay the shredded carrots and pineapple over the Jell-O without stirring it. Place it in the fridge for at least 1 h then serve it.

- Enjoy.

SERVINGS: 4

Preparation 10 mins- -**Total Time** 10 mins

NUTRITIONAL INFORMATION:

Calories 100.6, Fat 0.0g, Cholesterol 0.0mg, Sodium 111.3mg, Carbohydrates 24.1g, Protein 1.9g

CHEESY POTATO CASSEROLE

INGREDIENTS

- 8 C. raw **potatoes**, shredded

- 2 C. uncooked elbow **macaroni**

- 2 C. frozen **peas**

- 2 C. cooked **turkey**

- 3 tsp **salt**

- 1/2 C. **onion**, chopped

- 4 C. **cheese**, shredded

- 2 quarts **milk**

DIRECTIONS

- Before you do anything, preheat the oven to 325 F. Grease casserole dish and place it aside.

- Lay the shredded potato in the casserole then top it with the macaroni, peas, turkey, salt, onion, cheese and milk.

- Place the casserole in the oven and let it cook for 2 h 35 min.

- Serve it hot.

- Enjoy.

SERVINGS: 15

Preparation

NUTRITIONAL INFORMATION:

Calories 362.7, Fat 15.6g, Cholesterol 54.4mg, Sodium 857.9mg, Carbohydrates 36.1g, Protein 19.5g

COCONUT PUDDING

INGREDIENTS

- 2/3 C. **cracker** crumb

- 1/2 C. **sugar**

- 1 tbsp **flour**

- 1/2 C. **coconut**

- 1/2 tsp **salt**

- 2 1/2 C. sweet **milk**

DIRECTIONS

- Place a heavy saucepan over medium heat. Stir in it the cracker crumb with sugar, flour, coconut and salt.

- Stir into it 1/2 C. of milk. let them sit for a while.

- Heat the remaining milk. Add it to the mix and let them cook for 18 to 22 min while stirring all the time.

- Serve your pudding warm.

- Enjoy.

SERVINGS: 5

Preparation 15 mins- -**Total Time** 35 mins

NUTRITIONAL INFORMATION:

Calories 271.1, Fat 9.7g, Cholesterol 12.2mg, Sodium 288.8mg, Carbohydrates 41.1g, Protein 6.1g

SWEET MUSTARD DRESSING

INGREDIENTS

- 3/4 C. **oil**

- 1 **egg**

- 1 1/2 tsp **mustard**

- 2 tsp **salt**

- 1/3 C. **sugar**

- 1/2 C. **flour**

- 2 1/2 tbsp **flour**

- 1 1/3 C. **sugar**

- 1/3 C. **vinegar**

- 1 C. **water**

DIRECTIONS

- Get a large mixing bowl: Combine in it the oil, egg, mustard, salt and 1/3 C. sugar.

- Place a heavy saucepan over medium heat: Stir in it the flour, 1/3

- C. sugar, vinegar and water. Cook them until they start boiling.

- Keep them boiling until they become thick. Stir into the egg mix.

- Place the dressing in the fridge until it cools down completely then serve it.

- Enjoy.

SERVINGS: 1

Preparation 10 mins- -**Total Time** 20 mins

NUTRITIONAL INFORMATION:

Calories 1041.2, Fat 56.5g, Cholesterol 70.5mg, Sodium 1604.3mg, Carbohydrates 132.0g, Protein5.0g

HEN TART

INGREDIENTS

- FILLING

- 1 fat **hen**, cooked until tender 3 tbsp **butter**

- 3 tbsp **flour**

- 5 C. chicken **broth**

- 1 C. **milk**

- 2 -3 C. cooked mixed **peas carrots** and **potatoes** CRUST

- 2 C. **flour**

- 2 tsp **baking powder**

- 1 tsp **salt**

- 2 tbsp **shortening**

- 1 C. **milk**

- 1 **egg**

DIRECTIONS

- Before you do anything, preheat the oven to 425 F. Grease a pie dish and place it aside.

- Discard the bones from the chicken and shred it.

- Place a heavy saucepan over medium heat. Melt in it the butter.

- Add to it the flour and mix them well.

- Add the milk with broth gradually while whisking them all the time until they become creamy and thick.

- Stir the shredded chicken into the sauce.

- Get a large mixing bowl: Mix in it the shortening with baking powder, flour, and salt until you get a crumbly mixture. Mix in the egg.

- Pour the chicken mixture into the greased pie dish.4

- Roll the dough on a lightly floured surface and drape it over the chicken mixture. Use a sharp knife to cut long slits in it.

- Place the tart in the oven and let it cook for 28 to 32 min. Serve it warm.

- Enjoy.

SERVINGS: 1

Preparation 30 mins- -**Total Time** 2 hrs

NUTRITIONAL INFORMATION:

Calories 2782.7, Fat 139.5g, Cholesterol 685.2mg, Sodium 7609.5mg, Carbohydrates 238.5g, Protein 133.1g

BEEF BORCHT

INGREDIENTS

- 1 1/2-2 lbs **beef** stew meat, diced 1 **beef** bone

- 2 C. shredded **cabbage**

- 2 C. **potatoes**, cut in cubes

- 2 C. **beets**, chopped

- 2 C. cooked **tomatoes**

- 1/2 C. **carrot**, chopped

- 1 large **onion**, chopped

- 12 **peppercorns**

- 2 tbsp **dill** weed

- 2 **bay** leaves

- 2 -3 tsp sea **salt**

- 12 C. **water**

- 1 C. sour **cream**

DIRECTIONS

- Place a large pot over medium heat. Stir in it the meat and cover it with water. Put on the lid and cook it until it starts boiling.

- Lower the heat and let it cook for 1 h. Discard the grease on top of the meat broth.

- Stir the veggies into the meat pot with the spices. Stir in an extra 9 C. of water

- Put on the lid and cook them until they start boiling. Lower the heat and put on the lid.

- Let the stew cook for 35 min. Serve it hot.

- Enjoy.

SERVINGS: 1

Preparation 30 mins- -**Total Time** 2 hrs

NUTRITIONAL INFORMATION:

Calories 117.8, Fat 4.8g, Cholesterol 34.6mg, Sodium 364.9mg, Carbohydrates 8.5g, Protein 10.7g

SCALLOPED POTATO

INGREDIENTS

- 1/4 C. **butter**

- 2 tbsp all-purpose **flour**

- 1 1/2 C. nonfat **milk**

- 1 lb pasteurized **cheese**, cut into cubes 1 (16 oz.) packet frozen green **beans**, thawed 2 1/2 lbs **potatoes**, quartered 4 C. diced cooked **turkey**

- 1 tsp **onion** powder

- 1/2 tsp **salt**

- 1/2 tsp black **pepper**

DIRECTIONS

- Before you do anything, preheat the oven to 375 F. Grease a casserole dish and place it aside.

- Place a large saucepan over medium heat. Heat in it the butter until it melts.

- Mix into it the flour. Pour in the milk gradually while whisking them all the time.

- Stir in the cheese until it melts and mix becomes thick to make the white sauce.

- Add in the potato with beans, turkey, onion powder, salt and pepper. Pour the mix into the casserole dish.

- Place it in the oven and let it cook for 54 to 56 min. Serve it hot.

- Enjoy.

SERVINGS: 6

Preparation 30 mins

- Total Time

- 1 hr 30 mins

NUTRITIONAL INFORMATION:

Calories 762.7, Fat 42.4g, Cholesterol 154.6mg, Sodium 1085.1mg, Carbohydrates 49.6g, Protein 46.4g

FESTIVE BUTTERMILK BREAD

INGREDIENTS

- 1 C. **butter**, softened

- 2 C. **sugar**

- 2 large **eggs**

- 2 C. **buttermilk**

- 4 C. **flour**

- 2 tsp **baking soda**

- 2/3 C. **sugar**

- 2 tsp **cinnamon**

DIRECTIONS

- Before you do anything, preheat the oven to 350 F. Grease 2

- bread pans and place them aside.

- Get a large mixing bowl: Beat in it the butter, 2 C. of sugar and eggs until they become creamy.

- Mix in the milk, flour and baking soda. Pour half of the mix into the bread pans.

- Get a mixing bowl: Stir in it the cinnamon and 2/3 C. of sugar.

- Top the bread pans with 1/4 of the mix.

- Pour over it the remaining bread batter then top it with the remaining cinnamon and sugar mix.

- Place the bread pans in the oven and let them cook for 1 h. Allow them to cool down completely then serve them.

- Enjoy.

SERVINGS: 1

Preparation 15 mins- -**Total Time** 1 hr 5 mins

NUTRITIONAL INFORMATION:

Calories 2931.8, Fat 101.4g, Cholesterol 439.8mg, Sodium 2405.1mg, Carbohydrates 471.6g, Protein 41.2g

HASH BROWN LOAF

INGREDIENTS

- 4 large red **potatoes**

- 2 tbsp grated **onions**

- 1 tsp **salt**

- 1/4 tsp **pepper**

- 2 tbsp **butter**

- 2 tbsp **oil**

DIRECTIONS

- Bring a large salted pot of water to a boil. Cook in it the potatoes for 10 to 20 min or until they become soft.

- Get a food processor: Drain the potatoes and process them with the onion until they are well shredded.

- Get a large mixing bowl: Mix in it the potato and onion mix with salt, pepper.

- Place a large pan over medium heat. Heat in it the butter and oil.

- Pour into it the potato mix and spread it in the pan.

- Cook in it the hash brown loaf until it become golden brown on both sides. Serve it with your favorite toppings.

- Enjoy.

SERVINGS: 4

Preparation 20 mins- -**Total Time** 40 mins

NUTRITIONAL INFORMATION:

Calories 379.1, Fat 13.0g, Cholesterol 15.2mg, Sodium 644.6mg, Carbohydrates 59.2g, Protein 7.0g

CREAMY CORN CASSEROLE

INGREDIENTS

- 1 (18 oz.) cans creamed **corn**

- 2 **eggs**, beaten

- 2 tbsp granulated **sugar**

- 2 tbsp **butter**, softened

- 1 C. **milk**

- 2 tbsp **cornstarch**

DIRECTIONS

- Before you do anything, preheat the oven to 350 F. Grease a casserole dish and place it aside.

- Get a large mixing bowl: Whisk in it the eggs until they become frothy. Mix in it the sugar with corn.

- Place a heavy saucepan over medium heat. Heat in it the milk.

- Stir into it the cornstarch and butter. Mix them well.

- Stir the mix into the eggs and corn mixture. Pour the mix into the casserole and cook it in the oven for 46 to 48 min.

- Serve your corn casserole warm with some cornbread.

- Enjoy.

SERVINGS: 4

Preparation 1 hr- -**Total Time** 2 hrs

NUTRITIONAL INFORMATION:

Calories 265.8, Fat 11.0g, Cholesterol 129.5mg, Sodium 500.1mg, Carbohydrates 38.0g, Protein 7.6g

CARAMEL DELIGHT

INGREDIENTS

- 2 **pie shells**

- 3 C. brown **sugar**

- 3 C. **water**

- 2 tbsp **butter**

- 1 C. **flour**

- 3 C. **milk**

- 6 **egg** yolks

DIRECTIONS

- Place a heavy saucepan over medium heat: Stir in it the brown sugar, water and butter. Cook them until they start boiling. Keep the mix cooking for 3 to 4 min.

- Add to them the flour and mix them well. Cook them mix until ot starts boiling again. Turn off the heat and let it sit for 6 min.

- Pour the filling into 2 pie crusts. Place them in the fridge and let them chill until ready to serve.

- Enjoy.

SERVINGS: 8

Preparation 10 mins

NUTRITIONAL INFORMATION:

Calories 488.8, Fat 9.4g, Cholesterol 162.0mg, Sodium 105.0mg, Carbohydrates 96.8g, Protein 6.4g

JUICY APPLE PIES

INGREDIENTS

- 2 C. dried **apples**

- 2 C. cold **water**

- 1 pinch **salt**

- 2 C. **sugar**

- 1 **orange**, juice and grated rind 1 tbsp **cinnamon**

- 1 double crust pie **pastry**

DIRECTIONS

- Before you do anything, preheat the oven to 450 F.

- Place a heavy saucepan over medium heat. Combine in it the water with apples and salt. Let them cook until they become soft.

- Stir in the sugar, orange and cinnamon. Let them cook until the water vaporizes.

- Lay the pie pastry on a lightly floured surface. Slice it into 8

- inches circles.

- Divide the filling between the circles and place it on the far side of them. Roll the dough over the filling to the end.

- Press the edges to seal them and place them on a lined up baking sheet. Place the tarts in the oven and let them cook for 38 to 42 min.

- Allow the tarts to cool down completely then serve them.

- Enjoy.

SERVINGS: 1

Preparation 30 mins

NUTRITIONAL INFORMATION:

Calories 492.5, Fat 10.1g, Cholesterol 0.0mg, Sodium 208.5mg, Carbohydrates 102.6g, Protein 2.3g

CINNAMON COOKIES

INGREDIENTS

- 1 1/2 C. **sugar**

- 1 C. **shortening**

- 2 **eggs**

- 1 tsp **vanilla**

- 2 3/4 C. **flour**

- 1 tsp **baking soda**

- 1/2 tsp **salt**

- 2 tsp cream of **tartar**

- 1 tbsp **sugar**

- 1 tbsp **cinnamon**

DIRECTIONS

- Before you do anything, preheat the oven to 400 F. Line up a baking sheet.

- Get a large mixing bowl: Beet in it the shortening and sugar. Mix into them the eggs with vanilla.

- Get another mixing bowl: Stir in it the flour, baking soda, salt, and cream of tartar. Add to them the eggs mix and combine them well.

- Combine 1 tbsp of sugar and cinnamon in a shallow dish.

- Shape the dough into bite size pieces and roll them in the cinnamon mix.

- Place the balls on a lined up baking sheet. Cook them in the oven for 9 to 10 min. Allow them to cool down completely then serve them.

- Enjoy.

SERVINGS: 30

Preparation 15 mins- -**Total Time** 45 mins

NUTRITIONAL INFORMATION:

Calories 148.7, Fat 7.2g, Cholesterol 14.1mg, Sodium 85.7mg, Carbohydrates 19.5g, Protein 1.6g

ROLLED WALNUTS TART

INGREDIENTS

- 1 (8 inch) unbaked **pie shells** 1/2 C. **butter**, melted

- 3/4 C. brown **sugar**

- 2 **eggs**

- 3/4 C. light **corn syrup**

- 3/4 C. rolled **oats**

- 1/2 C. **walnut** pieces

DIRECTIONS

- Before you do anything, preheat the oven to 350 F. Grease a pie dish and lay the pie shell in it then place it aside.

- Get a large mixing bowl: Beat in it the sugar with melted butter until they become smooth.

- Add to them the eggs with corn syrup, oats and walnuts. Pour the filling into the pie shell.

- Place the pie in the oven and let it cook for 1 h. Allow it to cool down completely then serve it with your favorite toppings.

- Enjoy.

SERVINGS: 6

Preparation 10 mins

NUTRITIONAL INFORMATION:

Calories 621.8, Fat 32.9g, Cholesterol 111.1mg, Sodium 308.5mg, Carbohydrates 79.9g, Protein 7.0g

ALLSPICE TART

INGREDIENTS

- PIE

- 3 large **egg** yolks

- 4 tbsp all-purpose **flour**

- 1 C. brown **sugar**, packed

- 1/8 tsp **salt**

- 1 tsp ground **allspice**

- 1/4 tsp **mace**

- 1/4 C. cider **vinegar**

- 2 C. warm **water**

- 1/4 C. **butter**, softened

- 1 (9 inch) baked **pie crusts** MERINGUE TOPPING

- 3 large **egg** whites

- 1/4 tsp **salt**

- 1 tsp cider **vinegar**

- 6 tbsp granulated **sugar**

- 1 1/2 tsp **cornstarch**

DIRECTIONS

- Before you do anything, preheat the oven to 325 F. Grease a pie dish and lay the pie crust in it then place it aside.

- Place a bowl on a double boiler. Whisk in it the egg yolks until they become pale.

- Add to them the flour, sugar, salt and spices. Mix them well. Stir in the vinegar and warm water.

- Let the mixture cook for 26 min over simmering water until the batter becomes thick.

- Once the time is up, stir the butter into the batter until it melts. Let

- it cook for an extra 18 min.

- Once the time is up, spoon the mix into the pie crust. Place it aside to lose heat.

- Get a large mixing bowl: Cream in it the egg whites, salt and vinegar until its soft peaks.

- Mix into it the sugar gradually by 1 tbsp at a time followed by the cornstarch while maintaining the soft peak.

- Spoon the mix over the tart filling. Place it in the oven and let it cook for 7 to 9 min.

- Allow the tart to lose heat completely then serve it.

- Enjoy.

SERVINGS: 6

Preparation 15 mins- -**Total Time** 50 mins

NUTRITIONAL INFORMATION:

Calories 466.5, Fat 20.0g, Cholesterol 125.2mg, Sodium 404.0mg, Carbohydrates 67.1g, Protein 5.6g

GLAZED CRISCO PUFFS

INGREDIENTS

- 9 C. cake **flour**

- 1 tsp **salt**

- 3 C. Crisco **shortening**

- 2 tbsp **sugar**

- 2 C. **water**

- GLAZE

- 4 lbs powdered **sugar**

- 1/4 C. **cornstarch**

- 3 tbsp evaporated **milk**

- 1/2 tsp **vanilla**

- 1 1/4 C. **water**

DIRECTIONS

- Get a large mixing bowl: Combine in it the cake flour with salt, sugar and water until you get a dough.

- Roll the dough on a lightly floured surface. Cut it into circles of the size you desire. Place a 1 tbsp of the filling you want on the side of each circle.

- Pull the dough over the filling and press the edges to seal them.

- Place a deep pan over medium heat. Melt in it the shortening.

- Cook in it the puffs until they become golden brown.

- Drain them and place them aside.

- Get a mixing bowl: Mix in it the powdered sugar with cornstarch, milk, vanilla and water to make the glaze.

- Drizzle the glaze over the puffs then serve them.

- Enjoy.

SERVINGS: 1

Preparation 30 mins- -**Total Time** 35 mins

NUTRITIONAL INFORMATION:

Calories 431.1, Fat 15.7g, Cholesterol 0.3mg, Sodium 60.9mg, Carbohydrates 70.7g, Protein 2.6g

VALENTINE STRAWBERRY AMISH BREAD

INGREDIENTS

- 1 1/2 C. Amish **starter**, see appendix 3 **eggs**

- 1/2 C. **oil**

- 1/2 C. **applesauce**

- 1/2 C. **buttermilk**

- 2 (1/3 oz.) box sugar-free strawberry **gelatin mix** 1/4 C. **sugar**

- 2 C. **flour**

- 1 1/2 tsp **baking powder**

- 1/2 tsp **baking soda**

- 1/2 tsp **salt**

- 1 1/2 C. sliced **strawberries**

- 1 tbsp **sugar**

DIRECTIONS

- Before you do anything, preheat the oven to 325 F. Grease 5

- small bread pans and place them aside.

- Get a large mixing bowl: Whisk in it the Amish starter with eggs, oil, applesauce, and buttermilk well.

- Get a mixing bowl: Add to it the gelatin mix with sugar, flour, baking powder, baking soda, and salt. Mix them well.

- Get another mixing bowl: Stir in it the strawberries with 1 tbsp of sugar. Fold it into the batter.

- Pour the batter into the greased pan. Place them in the oven and let them cook for 48 min.

- Allow the bread pans to cool down completely then serve them.

- Enjoy.

SERVINGS: 10

Preparation 15 mins- -**Total Time** 1 hr

NUTRITIONAL INFORMATION:

Calories 239.7, Fat 12.8g, Cholesterol 63.9mg, Sodium 287.4mg, Carbohydrates 26.8g, Protein 5.3g

SPICY ORANGE BREAD

INGREDIENTS

- 1 1/2 C. Amish **starter**, see appendix 3 **eggs**

- 1/2 C. **oil**

- 1/2 C. **applesauce**

- 1/2 C. **orange** juice

- 1 (1/3 oz.) box sugar-free orange **Jell-O mix** 1/2 C. **sugar**

- 2 C. **flour**

- 1 1/2 tsp **baking powder**

- 1/2 tsp **baking soda**

- 1 1/2 tsp **allspice**

- 1/2 tsp **cinnamon**

- 1/2 tsp **salt**

- 1 C. dried **cranberries**

- 1 tbsp **orange** zest

- 1 C. **pecans**

DIRECTIONS

- Before you do anything, preheat the oven to 350 F. Grease 5

- small bread pans and place them aside.

- Get a large mixing bowl: Whisk in it the starter with eggs, oil, applesauce, and orange juice.

- Mix in it the orange Jell-O with flour, sugar, baking powder, baking soda, allspice, cinnamon and salt.

- Fold into them the cranberries with orange zest and pecans. Pour the batter into the pans. Cook them in the oven for 48 min.

- Allow them to cool down completely then serve them.

- Enjoy.

SERVINGS: 15

Preparation 20 mins

NUTRITIONAL INFORMATION:

Calories 179.8, Fat 8.4g, Cholesterol 42.3mg, Sodium 172.8mg, Carbohydrates 23.2g, Protein 3.1g

POPPY BREAD

INGREDIENTS

- 1 C. hot **water**

- 1 C. Amish **starter**, see appendix 1 tbsp **oil**

- 2 tbsp brown **sugar**

- 2 tsp **salt**

- 2 C. bread **flour**

- 1 1/2 C. wheat **flour**

- 2 tsp active dry **yeast**

- Mix

- 1 tbsp **rye** flakes

- 1 tbsp **wheat** flakes

- 1 tbsp whole **oat groats**

- 1 tbsp **millet**

- 1 tbsp **flax** seed

- 1 tbsp **poppy** seed

- 1 tbsp **sesame** seeds

- 1 tbsp **sunflower** seeds

DIRECTIONS

- Combine all the ingredients in a bread machine by following the instructions of the manufacturer.

- Select the French bread setting and let it cook.

- Enjoy.

SERVINGS: 12

Preparation

NUTRITIONAL INFORMATION:

Calories 160.7, Fat 3.1g, Cholesterol 0.0mg, Sodium 391.1mg, Carbohydrates 28.7g, Protein 5.2g

SPLENDA MUFFINS

INGREDIENTS

- **cooking spray**
- 3/4 C. yellow **cornmeal**
- 1/4 tsp **salt**
- 1/2 tsp **baking soda**
- 1 tbsp Splenda artificial **sweetener** 1 **egg**, beaten
- 3/4 C. **milk**
- 1/2 C. Amish **starter**, see appendix 2 tbsp **butter**, melted

DIRECTIONS

- Before you do anything, preheat the oven to 375 F. Grease 12 C.
- muffin tin and place it aside.
- Get a large mixing bowl: Mix in it the cornmeal, salt, baking soda and Splenda.
- Get another mixing bowl: Whisk in it the eggs, milk, starter and melted butter. Add to them the cornmeal mix while stirring them all the time.
- Pour the batter into the greased muffin tin. Place it in the oven and let it cook for 40 to 50 min.
- Allow them to cool down completely then serve them.
- Enjoy.

SERVINGS: 12

Preparation 40 mins- -**Total Time** 1 hr

NUTRITIONAL INFORMATION:

Calories 60.4, Fat 3.1g, Cholesterol 24.8mg, Sodium 130.4mg, Carbohydrates 6.6g, Protein 1.6g

NUTTY CARROT MUFFINS

INGREDIENTS

- 3/4 C. Amish **starter**, see appendix 1 **egg**, beaten

- 1/2 C. **buttermilk**

- 1/2 C. pureed **sweet potato** 1 tsp **vanilla**

- 1/2 C. fiber **cereal**

- 1/2 C. **oats**

- 1 tsp **salt**

- 2 tbsp Splenda artificial **sweetener** 1 tbsp brown **sugar**

- 1 1/2 C. **flour**

- 1 tsp **baking soda**

- 1/2 C. shredded **carrot**

- 1/2 C. **raisins**

- 1/2 C. chopped **walnuts**

DIRECTIONS

- Before you do anything, preheat the oven to 375 F. Grease 12 C.

- muffin pan and place it aside.

- Get a large mixing bowl: Cream in it the starter with vanilla, egg, sweet potato, and buttermilk.

- Mix in the cereal with oats, salt, Splenda, brown sugar, flour, and baking soda. Fold the carrot with raisins and walnuts into the batter.

- Pour the batter into the muffin pan. Place it in the oven and let it cook for 25 to 30 min.

- Allow them to cool down completely then serve them.

- Enjoy.

SERVINGS: 14

Preparation 10 mins- -**Total Time** 30 mins

NUTRITIONAL INFORMATION:

Calories 132.2, Fat 3.7g, Cholesterol 15.4mg, Sodium 276.9mg, Carbohydrates 21.3g, Protein 3.9g

JUNIPER STIR FRY

INGREDIENTS

- 1/4 C. walnut **oil**

- 1 tbsp white **mustard** seeds

- 1 medium **onion**, sliced

- 1 C. **chicken** stock

- 1 lb **sauerkraut**, drained

- 1 1/2 tbsp **ginger**, minced

- 7 -8 juniper **berries**

- 1 1/2 tbsp red bell **peppers**, chopped

DIRECTIONS

- Place a heavy saucepan over medium heat. Heat the oil in it. Stir in the mustard seeds and cook them for 40 sec.

- Mix in the onion and let it cook for 12 min over low heat with the lid on. Mix in the stock, sauerkraut, ginger, and juniper berries.

- Put on the lid and let them cook for 60 min. Serve your stir fry with bell pepper.

- Enjoy.

SERVINGS: 6

Preparation 10 mins

NUTRITIONAL INFORMATION:

Calories 130.8, Fat 10.3g, Cholesterol 1.2mg, Sodium 558.4mg, Carbohydrates 8.2g, Protein 2.4g

HOT CORNMEAL

INGREDIENTS

- 3 C. **water**

- 1 C. **cornmeal**

- 1 tsp **salt**

DIRECTIONS

- Grease a baking pan and place it aside.

- Place a large saucepan over medium heat. Stir in the water with cornmeal and salt. Put on the lid and let it cook for 15 to 20 min or until it is done.

- Pour the mixture into the greased pan. Place it aside let it sit unit it lose heat completely. Slice it into squares.

- Place a large pan over medium heat. Heat in it a splash of oil.

- Cook in it the corn squares until they become golden brown then serve them.

- Enjoy.

SERVINGS: 8

Preparation 5 mins- -**Total Time** 25 mins

NUTRITIONAL INFORMATION:

Calories 55.2, Fat 0.5g, Cholesterol 0.0mg, Sodium 298.6mg, Carbohydrates 11.7g, Protein 1.2g

SLOW BURGER STEW

INGREDIENTS

- 2 C. **hamburger**

- 2 C. sliced raw **potatoes**

- 2 C. chopped **celery**

- 1/2 C. diced **onion**

- 2 tsp **salt**

- 1/4 tsp **pepper**

- 1 C. diced green **pepper**

- 2 C. canned **tomatoes**

DIRECTIONS

- Combine all the ingredients in a slow cooker. Put on the lid and let them cook for 7 h on low. Serve it hot.

- Enjoy.

SERVINGS: 4

Preparation

NUTRITIONAL INFORMATION:

Calories 102.0, Fat 0.4g, Cholesterol 0.0mg, Sodium 1381.1mg, Carbohydrates 23.0g, Protein 3.3g

CREAMY JELL-O AND EGG SALAD

INGREDIENTS

- 8 oz. cream **cheese**, softened 1 C. **celery**, cut

- 1 C. **cucumber**, cut

- 1 small **onion**, cut

- 3 **eggs**, hard-boiled, cut

- 3 tbsp **mayonnaise**

- 3 oz. lemon Jell-O **gelatin**

DIRECTIONS

- Get a large mixing bowl: Toss in it the celery, cucumber and onion.

- Get another mixing bowl: Mix in it 1 C. of boiling water with Jell-O. Place it aside to cool down.

- Get a small mixing bowl: beat in it the mayonnaise with cream cheese until it become smooth. Add it to the veggies with Jell-O

- and a pinch of salt.

- Toss them to coat. Place the salad in the fridge and let it sit until ready to serve.

- Enjoy.

SERVINGS: 16

Preparation 10 mins

NUTRITIONAL INFORMATION:

Calories 97.9, Fat 6.8g, Cholesterol 55.9mg, Sodium 104.7mg, Carbohydrates 6.7g, Protein 2.8g

CHICKEN FARM SOUP

INGREDIENTS

- 12 C. **water**

- 2 lbs boneless skinless **chicken** breasts, cubed 1 C. chopped **onion**

- 1 C. chopped **celery**

- 1 C. shredded **carrot**

- 3 chicken **bouillon** cubes

- 2 (14 3/4 oz.) cans cream-style **corn** 2 C. uncooked egg **noodles**

- 1/4 C. **butter**

- 1 tsp **salt**

- 1/4 tsp **pepper**

DIRECTIONS

- Place a large pot over medium heat. Stir in it the water, chicken, onion, celery, carrots and bouillon.

- Cook them until they start boiling. Lower the heat and let them cook for 35 min.

- Once the time is up, add the corn, noodles and butter to the pot.

- Let them cook for 12 min.

- Adjust the seasoning of the soup then serve it hot.

- Enjoy.

SERVINGS: 16

Preparation 15 mins- -**Total Time** 55 mins

NUTRITIONAL INFORMATION:

Calories 153.7, Fat 4.1g, Cholesterol 44.6mg, Sodium 505.8mg, Carbohydrates 14.8g, Protein 15.0g

CREAMY CHICKEN ROAST

INGREDIENTS

- 1 cut-up roasting **chicken**

- 1/2 C. **flour**

- 1 tsp **salt**

- 1 dash **pepper**

- 3 tbsp **butter**

- 1 1/2 C. **cream**

DIRECTIONS

- Before you do anything, preheat the oven to 350 F.

- Get a large mixing bowl: Stir in it the flour, salt, and pepper.

- Place a large pan over medium heat. Heat the butter in it until it melts.

- Dust the chicken pieces with the flour mix then cook them in the melted butter until they become golden brown.

- Drain them and transfer them to a baking pan. Drizzle the cream all over the chicken pieces. Cook them in the oven for 2 h.

- Serve your creamy chicken roast hot.

- Enjoy.

SERVINGS: 6

Preparation 20 mins

NUTRITIONAL INFORMATION:

Calories 368.8, Fat 32.0g, Cholesterol 117.2mg, Sodium 492.0mg, Carbohydrates 9.7g , Protein 10.8g

APPLESAUCE MUFFINS

INGREDIENTS

- 1 1/2 C. boiling **water**

- 1 tsp **baking soda**

- 1 C. dark **molasses**

- 3 C. **flour**

- 1 C. brown **sugar**, packed

- 1/4 C. **butter**

- 1/4 C. unsweetened **applesauce**

DIRECTIONS

- Before you do anything, preheat the oven to 350 F. line up a muffin pan with Cake liners.

- Get a large mixing bowl: Stir in the boiling water with soda. Stir in the molasses and place it aside.

- Get a mixing bowl: Mix in in it the flour, brown sugar and margarine until you get a crumbly mix. Place 1 C. of it aside.

- Add the applesauce the rest of the crumble mix and combine them well. Pour the batter into the muffin C.. Top it with the remaining 1 C. of crumbs.

- Place the pan in the oven and let it cook for 22 to 26 min.

- Enjoy.

SERVINGS: 1

Preparation 20 mins- -**Total Time** 45 mins

NUTRITIONAL INFORMATION:

Calories 150.4, Fat 2.0g, Cholesterol 5.0mg, Sodium 77.8mg, Carbohydrates 31.7g, Protein 1.6g

VANILLA COFFEE CAKE

INGREDIENTS

- 2 C. light brown **sugar**

- 2 C. all-purpose **flour**

- 3/4 C. **shortening**

- 1 **egg**

- 2 tsp **vanilla** extract

- 1 C. hot strong **coffee**

- 1 tsp **baking soda**

DIRECTIONS

- Before you do anything, preheat the oven to 325 F. Grease a cake pan and place it aside.

- Get a large mixing bowl: Combine it the sugar, flour and shortening until they become crumbly.

- Stir the baking soda into the coffee. Pour it into the flour bowl and mix them well.

- Mix in the egg and vanilla. Pour the batter into the greased pan.

- Place it in the oven and let it cook for 32 min.

- Allow the cake to cool down completely then serve it with your favorite toppings.

- Enjoy.

SERVINGS: 6

Preparation 10 mins- -**Total Time** 40 mins

NUTRITIONAL INFORMATION:

Calories 671.0, Fat 26.8g, Cholesterol 35.2mg, Sodium 251.7mg, Carbohydrates 103.4g, Protein 5.4g

BANANA CAKE WITH VANILLA FROSTING

INGREDIENTS

- CAKE

- 2/3 C. **vegetable** shortening

- 1 2/3 C. **sugar**

- 3 whole **eggs**, room temp

- 2 1/4 C. all-purpose **flour**

- 1 1/4 tsp **baking powder**

- 1 1/4 tsp **baking soda**

- 1 1/4 tsp **salt**

- 2/3 C. **buttermilk**

- 1 1/4 C. **bananas**, mashed

- 2/3 C. chopped black **walnut**

- PENUCHE FROSTING

- 3/4 C. **butter**

- 1 1/2 C. brown **sugar**

- 1/4 C. **milk**, plus

- 2 tbsp **milk**

- 1/2 tsp **salt**

- 1 1/2 tsp **vanilla** extract

- 3 C. powdered **sugar**

DIRECTIONS

- Before you do anything, preheat the oven to 350 F. Grease a 2

- cake pans and place them aside.

- Get a large mixing bowl: Beat in it the sugar with shortening until they become light. Beat in the eggs gradually.

- Mix in the sugar with flour, baking powder, baking soda, and salt.

- Add the buttermilk and combine them well until you get a smooth batter.

- Gold the banana and walnuts into the batter. Pour it into the cake pans and cook them for 36 to 42 min in the oven.

- Place a heavy saucepan over medium heat: Combine in it the brown sugar with butter until they melt. Cook them until they start boiling.

- Lower the heat and let them cook for an extra 2 to 3 min while stirring all the time. Mix in the milk and cook them until they start boiling while stirring all the time.

- Get a large mixing bowl: Pour in it the hot milk mix with vanilla and a pinch of salt.

- Add to them the powdered sugar gradually while beating them until they become smooth and creamy to make the frosting.

- Allow the cakes to cool down completely Spread the frosting all over them. Place them in the fridge until ready to serve.

- Enjoy.

SERVINGS: 12

Preparation 30 mins

NUTRITIONAL INFORMATION:

Calories 700.7, Fat 28.8g, Cholesterol 78.6mg, Sodium 635.0mg, Carbohydrates 107.8g, Protein 6.4g

VANILLA BLONDIES

INGREDIENTS

- 1/4 C. **butter**

- 1 C. brown **sugar**

- 1 **egg**

- 1 C. all-purpose **flour**

- 1 tsp **vanilla**

- 1/2 tsp **salt**

- 1 tsp **baking powder**

DIRECTIONS

- Before you do anything, preheat the oven to 350 F. Grease a cake pan and place it aside.

- Place a heavy saucepan over medium heat. Heat in it the butter until it melts. Mix in the sugar and keep stirring them until they melt.

- Turn off the heat and allow the mix to lose heat completely.

- Combine in the egg, flour, vanilla, salt, and baking powder. Beat them until they become smooth.

- Pour the batter into the cake pan. Cook it in the oven for 32 min.

- Allow it to cool down completely then cut it into squares. Serve your brownies or store them in the fridge.

- Enjoy.

SERVINGS: 1

Preparation 40 mins

NUTRITIONAL INFORMATION:

Calories 222.4, Fat 6.5g, Cholesterol 41.6mg, Sodium 251.4mg, Carbohydrates 38.9g, Protein 2.4g

AMISH MINT TEA

INGREDIENTS

- 4 quarts **water**, boiling

- 1 quart meadow mint **tea**, stems & leaves 4 -6 C. **sugar**

DIRECTIONS

- Pour 4 quarts of water in a kettle. Heat them until they start boiling.

- Stir in 1 quart of tea stems and leaves. Heat them again until they start boiling.

- Once the time is up, turn the heat off and let the tea sit for 1 h while pressing it every once in a while.

- Once the time is up, discard the leaves and stems. Use a fine cheesecloth to strain the tea.

- Pour the tea in a heavy saucepan. Stir into 5 C. of sugar and heat it until it dissolves.

- Let it cool down completely then freeze it until ready to use.

- To serve your tea, Stir 1 concentrate box of it with 2 to 3 water concentrate boxes.

- Enjoy.

SERVINGS: 1

Preparation 15 mins- -**Total Time** 45 mins

NUTRITIONAL INFORMATION:

Calories

309.7, Fat 0.0g, Cholesterol 0.0mg, Sodium 7.9mg, Carbohydrates 80.0g, Protein 0.0g

CRUNCHY BROCCOLI WITH CHEDDAR SAUCE

INGREDIENTS

broccoli

- 2 C. chopped **onions**

- 4 tbsp **flour**

- 1 tsp **salt**

- 2 C. **milk**

- 1/4 lb mild cheddar **cheese**

DIRECTIONS

- Before you do anything, preheat the oven to 375 F. Grease a baking pan.

- Bring a large pot of water and a pinch of salt to a boil. Stir in it the broccoli and let it cook for 8 min.

- Place a heavy saucepan over medium heat: Melt in it the butter.

- Add the flour and mix it well.

- Add the milk gradually while whisking all the time until you get a smooth and thick mix. Stir in the cheese until it melts to make the sauce.

- Toss half of the broccoli with onion in the baking pan. Drizzle over it half of the cheese sauce.

- Top it with the remaining half of the broccoli then drizzle the cheese sauce over it. Place the pan in the oven and let it cook for 48 min.

- Serve your broccoli casserole warm.

- Enjoy.

SERVINGS: 4

Preparation 10 mins- -**Total Time** 55 mins

NUTRITIONAL INFORMATION:

Calories 252.9, Fat 14.0g, Cholesterol 46.9mg, Sodium 820.8mg, Carbohydrates 19.4g, Protein 12.7g

CONDENSED MAPLE TART

INGREDIENTS

- 1 (14 oz.) cans condensed **milk**

- 2/3 C. real maple **syrup**

- 1 pinch **salt**

- 9 inches baked **pie shells whipped** cream

DIRECTIONS

- Place a heavy saucepan over low heat. Stir in it the maple syrup, condensed milk and the pinch of salt.

- Cook them until bubbles starts forming while stirring all the time to make the filling. Turn off the heat and let it lose heat for a while.

- Pour the filling into the pie shell. Place it in the fridge and let it sit for 3 h in the fridge.

- Once the time is up, garnish it with some whipped cream then serve it.

- Enjoy.

SERVINGS: 1

Preparation 2 mins- -**Total Time** 22 mins

NUTRITIONAL INFORMATION:

Calories 2826.6, Fat 96.9g, Cholesterol 143.6mg, Sodium 1646.0mg, Carbohydrates 455.9g, Protein 44.4g

SALISBURY STEAK WITH MUSHROOM SAUCE

INGREDIENTS

- 1 lb ground **beef**

- 1 C. **milk**

- 1 C. **cracker** crumb

- 1/4 tsp **pepper**

- 1 tsp **salt**

- 1 small **onion**, chopped

- 1 can **mushroom** soup

- 1 C. **water**

DIRECTIONS

- Get a large mixing bowl: Combine in it the beef with cracker crumb, onion, salt and pepper well. Shape the mix into a slightly flat meatloaf.

- Wrap it in a piece of plastic wrap and place it in the fridge for an overnight.

- Before you do anything, preheat the oven to 325 F. Grease a casserole dish.

- Once the time is up, slice meatloaf into thin pieces.

- Place a skillet over medium heat. Heat a splash of oil in it. Cook in it the meatloaf slices for 4 min until they become golden.

- Drain the beef slices and transfer them to the casserole dish. Stir into them the mushroom soup with milk and water.

- Place the casserole in the oven and let it cook for 1 h. Serve it hot.

- Enjoy.

SERVINGS: 4

Preparation 8 hrs- -**Total Time** 9 hrs

NUTRITIONAL INFORMATION:

Calories 433.6, Fat 21.4g, Cholesterol 85.6mg, Sodium 1045.7mg, Carbohydrates 31.7g, Protein 26.6g

QUICK CORN AND EGG SOUP

INGREDIENTS

- 2 C. **flour**

- 1/2 tsp **salt**

- 1 **egg**, beaten

- 1 1/2-2 quarts **chicken** broth 1 (15 1/4 oz.) cans **corn**, drained and crushed

DIRECTIONS

- Get a large mixing bowl: Mix in it the flour, salt and beaten egg until they become crumbly.

- Place a large saucepan over medium heat. Pour in it the broth and heat it through.

- Stir in the corn and cook them until they start simmering. Mix in the flour mix.

- Let them soup cook for 12 min while stirring from time to time.

- Adjust the seasoning of the soup then serve it hot.

- Enjoy.

SERVINGS: 4

Preparation 5 mins- -**Total Time** 20 mins

NUTRITIONAL INFORMATION:

Calories 407.7, Fat 5.5g, Cholesterol 46.5mg, Sodium 1430.7mg, Carbohydrates 71.8g, Protein 19.1g

SWEET SPICY RAISINS SAUCE

INGREDIENTS

- 2 C. **water**

- 1 C. **sugar**

- 1 tbsp **vinegar**

- 1 tbsp unsalted **butter**

- 1 1/2 C. **raisins**

- 1/4 tsp **salt**

- 1 tbsp **cinnamon**

- THICKENING MIXTURE

- 1 C. **water**

- 1/8 C. **cornstarch**

DIRECTIONS

- Place a heavy saucepan over medium heat. Stir in it the sugar with vinegar, 2 C. of water, butter, raisins, salt and cinnamon.

- Cook them until they start boiling. Lower the heat.

- Get a small mixing bowl: Whisk in it the cornstarch with water.

- Stir them into the raisins mix. Let them cook until they sauce become slightly thick.

- Serve your sauce hot with roast chicken, turkey, meatloaf Enjoy.

SERVINGS: 4

Preparation 5 mins- -**Total Time** 20 mins

NUTRITIONAL INFORMATION:

Calories 401.8, Fat 3.1g, Cholesterol 7.6mg, Sodium 156.1mg, Carbohydrates 98.0g, Protein 1.7g

RHUBARB ROLLS WITH VANILLA SAUCE

INGREDIENTS

- SAUCE

- 1 1/2 C. **sugar**

- 1 tbsp **flour**

- 1/2 tsp **cinnamon**

- 1/4 tsp **salt**

- 1 1/2 C. **water**

- 1/3 C. **margarine**

- 1 tsp **vanilla** extract

- red food **coloring**

- DOUGH

- 2 C. **flour**

- 2 tbsp **sugar**

- 2 tsp **baking powder**

- 1/4 tsp **salt**

- 2 1/2 tbsp cold **butter**

- 3/4 C. **milk**

- FILLING

- 2 tbsp **butter**, softened

- 2 C. chopped **rhubarb**

- 1/2 tsp **cinnamon**

- 1/2 C. **sugar**

DIRECTIONS

- To make the sauce:

- Before you do anything, preheat the oven to 350 F. Grease a cake pan and place it aside.

- Place a heavy saucepan over medium heat. Stir in it the sugar, flour, cinnamon, salt, butter and water.

- Cook them until they start boiling. let them cook for an extra 2 min.

- Turn off the heat then stir in the vanilla with food coloring. Place it aside to cool down.

- To make the dough:

- Get a large mixing bowl: Mix in it the sugar, flour, baking powder, butter and salt until they become crumbly.

- Mix in the milk until you get a dough. Place it on a floured surface and roll it until it is 13x9.

- Get a small mixing bowl: Stir in it the cinnamon and sugar.

- Place the softened butter over the whole dough. Lay over it the rhubarb and top it with the cinnamon and sugar mix.

- Roll the dough over the filling then cut it into 12 rolls. Place the rolls with the open sides facing up in the cake pan.

- Pour the vanilla sauce all over them. Place the pan in the oven and let them cook for 36 to 42 min.

- Serve your rhubarb rolls warm.

- Enjoy.

SERVINGS: 1

Preparation 20 mins- -**Total Time** 55 mins

NUTRITIONAL INFORMATION:

Calories 438.0, Fat 11.4g, Cholesterol 20.3mg, Sodium 352.5mg, Carbohydrates 80.8g, Protein 4.4g

CARAMEN PECAN CAKE

INGREDIENTS

- CAKE

- 1/2 C. **pecans**, chopped

- 2 1/2 C. cooking **apples**, chopped 1/2 C. **butter**, softened

- 1 C. granulated **sugar**

- 1 **egg**

- 1 tsp **baking soda**

- 1/4 tsp **salt**

- 1 tsp ground **cinnamon**

- 1 tsp grated **nutmeg**

- 1 C. **flour**

- CARAMEL SAUCE

- 3/4 C. **butter**

- 1 1/2 C. brown **sugar**

- 3/4 tsp **salt**

- 1 1/2 tsp **vanilla**

- 3/4 C. heavy **cream**

DIRECTIONS

- Before you do anything, preheat the oven to 350 F. Grease a cake pan and place it aside.

- Get a large mixing bowl: Beat in it the butter with sugar until they become light.

- Beat in it the egg until they become smooth followed by the baking soda, salt, cinnamon, and nutmeg.

- Add the flour and mix them well. Fold the nuts with apples into the batter.

- Pour the batter into the pan. Place it in the oven and let it cook for

- 32 min.

- In the meantime, place a heavy saucepan over medium heat. Stir in it the butter, brown sugar, and salt until they melt.

- Cook them until they start boiling while stirring all the time. Turn off the heat then stir in it the vanilla and the cream to make the caramel sauce.

- Allow it to cool down completely then serve it with the hot sauce.

- Enjoy.

SERVINGS: 8

Preparation 10 mins- -**Total Time** 40 mins

NUTRITIONAL INFORMATION:

Calories 722.6, Fat 42.8g, Cholesterol 130.0mg, Sodium 731.2mg, Carbohydrates 84.9g, Protein 3.9g

STARTER AMISH BISCUITS

INGREDIENTS

- 1 C. all-purpose **flour**
- 1/2 tsp **baking soda**
- 1/2 tsp **salt**
- 2 tsp **baking powder**
- 2 **eggs**, beaten
- 1 C. Amish **starter**, see appendix 1/4 C. vegetable **oil**
- 1/4 C. **butter**, melted

DIRECTIONS

- Before you do anything, preheat the oven to 350 F. Grease a baking sheet.
- Get a large mixing bowl: Stir in it the flour, baking soda, salt and baking powder.
- Get a mixing bowl: Beat in it the eggs, Amish Starter and oil until they become smooth.
- Add to them the flour mix and combine them well until you get dough.
- Flatten the dough with a rolling pin on a floured surface until it becomes 1/2 inch thick.
- Use a 3 inches cookie cutter to cut the dough into circles. Place the dough circles on the baking sheet.
- Coat the dough circles with melted butter. Lay over them a kitchen towel and let them sit for 35 min.
- Place the biscuits in the oven and cook them for 16 to 22 min.
- Allow it to cool down completely then serve them.
- Enjoy.

SERVINGS: 24

Preparation 0 mins- -**Total Time** 0 mins

NUTRITIONAL INFORMATION:

Calories 62.3, Fat 4.6g, Cholesterol 22.7mg, Sodium 124.4mg, Carbohydrates 4.1g, Protein 1.0g

ENDIVE SALAD WITH BACON DRESSING

INGREDIENTS

- SALAD

- 1 quart **endive**

- 3 hard-boiled **eggs**

- HOT BACON DRESSING

- **4 slices** turkey bacon

- 1/2 C. **sugar**

- 2 tbsp **flour**

- 1 **egg**, beaten

- 1 tsp **salt**

- 1/2 C. **vinegar**

- 1 1/2 C. **water**

DIRECTIONS

- Get a serving bowl: Lay in it the endive pieces. Lay over them the slices eggs.

- Place a saucepan over medium heat: Cook in it the bacon until it become crisp. Drain it and place it aside.

- Stir the flour with sugar into the saucepan and mix them well.

- Mix in it the egg, salt, vinegar and water until they become thick and creamy.

- Crumble the bacon and stir it into the dressing. Drizzle it over the eggs salad then serve it right away.

- Enjoy.

SERVINGS: 6

Preparation 15 mins- -**Total Time** 25 mins

NUTRITIONAL INFORMATION:

Calories 243.0, Fat 10.8g, Cholesterol 151.5mg, Sodium 616.4mg, Carbohydrates 28.0g, Protein 9.5g

HOMEMADE KETCHUP

INGREDIENTS

- 3 quarts **tomato** juice

- 1 pint apple cider **vinegar**

- 4 -5 C. **sugar**

- 1 tsp **salt**

- 1/4 tsp **pepper**

- 3 drops clove **oil**

- 5 drops cinnamon **oil**

- 4 tbsp ground dry **mustard**

DIRECTIONS

- Place a large saucepan over medium heat. Combine in it all the ingredients. Let them cook for 2 h 35 min.

- Allow it to cool down completely. Pour the mix into mason jars.

- Place them in them in the fridge until ready to serve.

- Enjoy.

SERVINGS: 1

Preparation

NUTRITIONAL INFORMATION:

Calories 352.9, Fat 0.9g, Cholesterol 0.0mg, Sodium 558.8mg, Carbohydrates 86.2g, Protein 1.5g

CLASSIC CHEESE CORN

INGREDIENTS

- 2 ears **corn**

- 1/2 C. Swiss **cheese**, diced

- 2 tsp **butter**, very soft

- 1 pinch cayenne **pepper**

- 1 pinch **salt**

DIRECTIONS

- Bring a large pot of water to a boil. Place in it the corn cobs and let them cook for 3 min.

- Once the time is up, drain them and pat them dry with some paper towels. Scrap the kernels from the cobs into a mixing bowl with a sharp knife.

- Stir in the butter with cheese and cayenne pepper into the corn kernels while they are hot.

- Adjust the seasoning of your salad then serve it right away.

- Enjoy.

SERVINGS: 1

Preparation 10 mins- -**Total Time** 12 mins

NUTRITIONAL INFORMATION:

Calories 527.6, Fat 25.6g, Cholesterol 69.8mg, Sodium 352.8mg, Carbohydrates 62.2g, Protein 22.4g

PEANUT CRACKERS

INGREDIENTS

- 1 C. brown **sugar**

- 1 C. light **molasses**

- 1 C. **water**

- 1 dash **salt**

- 4 tbsp **butter**

- 2 C. shelled **peanuts**

DIRECTIONS

- Line up and grease baking sheet.

- Place a saucepan over low heat: Stir in it the sugar, molasses, water and salt.

- Let them cook until they reach a temperature of 280 F.

- Mix in the butter until it melts. Turn off the heat and fold the peanuts into the mix.

- Pour the mix in the baking sheet. Place it aside until it cools down completely cools down and harden.

- Break it into pieces.

- Enjoy.

SERVINGS: 15

Preparation 25 mins

- Total Time

- 1 hr 25 mins

NUTRITIONAL INFORMATION:

Calories 257.9, Fat 12.6g, Cholesterol 8.1mg, Sodium 50.0mg, Carbohydrates 34.2g, Protein 5.0g

SWEET AND SALTY BEEF CHILI

INGREDIENTS

- 1 lb ground **beef**
- 1/2 C. chopped **onion**
- 1/2 C. chopped **celery**
- 3 tbsp **flour**
- 1/4 C. brown **sugar**
- 1/4 C. **ketchup**
- 4 C. **tomato** juice
- 2 -3 tbsp **chili** powder
- 16 oz. kidney **beans**
- **salt** and **pepper**

DIRECTIONS

- Place a large pot over medium heat. Cook in it the beef, onions and celery for 8 min. Discard the excess fat.
- Mix in the flour and cook them for 2 min. Stir in the sugar with ketchup, tomato juice, chili powder, beans, a pinch of salt and pepper.
- Put on the lid and let the stew cook for 32 min. Serve it hot.
- Enjoy.

SERVINGS: 6

Preparation 30 mins- -**Total Time** 1 hr

NUTRITIONAL INFORMATION:

Calories 326.5, Fat 12.3g, Cholesterol 51.4mg, Sodium 874.5mg, Carbohydrates 35.1g , Protein 20.3g

TROPICAL MARSHMALLOW DELIGHT

INGREDIENTS

- 16 **marshmallows**

- 1 C. **milk**

- 1 (3 oz.) packet lime **gelatin**

- 2 (4 oz.) packages cream **cheese**

- 1 (20 oz.) cans crushed **pineapple** 2/3 C. salad **dressing**

- 1 C. whipped **cream**

DIRECTIONS

- Get a large mixing bowl and place it on a double boiler. Stir in it the milk with marshmallows until they completely melt.

- Get a mixing bowl: Place in it the gelatin. Add to it the melted marshmallow mix and stir them well until it melts.

- Add the cream cheese and mix them well. Fold the pineapple into the mix and place it aside to lose heat completely.

- Fold the whipped cream and salad dressing into the mix. Place in it the fridge until it completely cools down then serve it.

- Enjoy.

SERVINGS: 1

Preparation 1 hr- -**Total Time** 1 hr

NUTRITIONAL INFORMATION:

Calories 2388.8, Fat 118.1g, Cholesterol 426.1mg, Sodium 2608.2mg, Carbohydrates 307.1g Protein45.2g

CHEESY BEEF AND NOODLES CASSEROLE

INGREDIENTS

- 2 lbs ground **beef**

- **salt** and **pepper**

- 2 tbsp brown **sugar**

- 1/4 C. chopped **onion**

- 1 can **tomato** soup

- 1 can cream of **chicken** soup

- 1 (16 oz.) packet egg **noodles**

- 1 (8 oz.) packet processed **cheese**

DIRECTIONS

- Before you do anything, preheat the oven to 350 F. Grease a baking pan and place it aside.

- Prepare the noodles by following the directions on the package.

- Place a large pot over medium heat. Cook in it the beef with salt, pepper, brown sugar and onion. Discard the excess fat.

- Stir in chicken soup. Pour the beef mix in the baking pan then top it with half of the cheese.

- Lay the noodles over it and sprinkle the remaining cheese on top.

- Place the pan in the oven and let it cook for 32 min.

- Serve your noodles casserole hot.

- Enjoy.

SERVINGS: 8

Preparation 10 mins- -**Total Time** 45 mins

NUTRITIONAL INFORMATION:

Calories 635.6, Fat 29.0g, Cholesterol 146.3mg, Sodium 1071.3mg, Carbohydrates 56.0g, Protein 36.5g

EASY AMISH FRIENDSHIP STARTER

INGREDIENTS

- 1 (.25 oz.) package active dry **yeast** 1/4 C. warm **water**

- 3 C. all-purpose **flour**, separated 3 C. white **sugar**, separated

- 3 C. **milk**

DIRECTIONS

- In a bowl, add the warm water and yeast and mix until well combined.

- Keep aside for about 9-10 minutes.

- In a ceramic container, add 1 C. of the sugar. and 1 C. of the flour and mix well.

- Gradually, add 1 C. of the milk and yeast mixture and mix until well combined.

- Cover the container loosely and ad keep aside until mixture becomes bubbly.

- Keep aside at room temperature for 10 days.

- Stir the starter on the 2nd and then 4th day well.

- On day 5; add 1 C. of the milk, 1 C. of the flour and 1 C. of the sugar and mix until well combined.

- From 6th to 9th day stir the mixture daily.

- On day 10; add 1 C. of the milk, 1 C. of the flour and 1 C. of the sugar and mix until well combined.

- Now, you can prepare the bread.

- Transfer the remaining starter in an airtight container and place in the fridge to preserve.

SERVINGS: 120

- -Total Time 9 d 40 m

NUTRITIONAL INFORMATION:

Calories 34, Fat 0.2g, Cholesterol < 1mg, Sodium 3mg, Carbohydrates 7.7g, Protein 0.5g

ALTERNATIVE 2-INGREDIENT AMISH STARTER

INGREDIENTS

- 700 g (24.5oz.) bread **flour**

- 700 g (24.5oz.) filtered **water**, separated in two parts

DIRECTIONS

- On day 1: in a container, add 70 g of the water and 70 g of the flour and mix well.

- With the lid, cover the container loosely and keep aside at 70

- degrees F temperature for about 24 hours.

- On day 2: add 70 g of the water and 70 g of the flour and mix well.

- With the lid, cover the container loosely and keep aside at 70

- degrees F temperature for about 24 hours.

- On day 3: with a spoon, remove half of the starter from the container.

- Add more 70 g of the water and 70 g of the flour and mix well.

- With the lid, cover the container loosely and keep aside at 70

- degrees F temperature for about 24 hours.

- From day 4 to day 10: repeat the process of day 3 daily until starter is fermented nicely.

- Place the container in the fridge until using.

- For the bread: place the container of starter at room temperature for about 2 days and repeat the process of day 3 daily.

- If you want to refrigerate the remaining starter then, add more 70

- g of the water and 70 g of the flour in 140 g of starter and mix.

- Refrigerate the starter until using.

SERVINGS: 120

- -**Total Time** 10 d 15 m

NUTRITIONAL INFORMATION:

Calories 316, Fat 1.5g, Cholesterol 0mg, Sodium 4mg, Carbohydrates 63.5g, Protein 10.5g

SUNNY CORNBREAD

INGREDIENTS

- 1 C. sifted **flour**

- 1/4 C. **sugar**

- 1 tbsp **baking powder**

- 3/4 tsp **salt**

- 1 C. yellow **cornmeal**

- 1 **egg**, well beaten

- 1 C. **milk**

- 5 tbsp **shortening**, melted and cooled

DIRECTIONS

- Before you do anything, preheat the oven to 425 F. Grease a loaf pan and place it aside.

- Get a large mixing bowl: Stir in it the flour with sugar, baking powder, salt and cornmeal.

- Get another mixing bowl: Whisk in it the milk with egg and shortening.

- Mix in the flour mix until they become smooth. Pour the batter into the loaf pan and cook it in the oven for 22 min.

- Allow the cornbread to sit for 5 min in the pan then place it aside to lose heat completely and serve it.

- Enjoy.

SERVINGS: 4

Preparation 10 mins- -**Total Time** 30 mins

NUTRITIONAL INFORMATION:

Calories 473.1, Fat 20.8g, Cholesterol 61.4mg, Sodium 767.0mg, Carbohydrates 63.5g, Protein 9.2g

CREAMY NOODLES AND BEEF CASSEROLE

INGREDIENTS

- 1 lb ground **beef**

- 1 **onion**, chopped

- 1/2 C. **celery**, chopped

- 1 tbsp **garlic**, minced

- 1 (14 oz.) cans diced **tomatoes**

- 1 (10 1/2 oz.) cans cream of **chicken** soup 1 (12 oz.) packet wide egg **noodles** 1/2 C. shredded cheddar **cheese**

DIRECTIONS

- Before you do anything, preheat the oven to 350 F. Grease a casserole dish and place it aside.

- Bring a large pot of water with a pinch of salt to a boil. Prepare in it the noodles according to the directions on the package.

- Place a large pan over medium heat Brown in it the beef with onion for 4 min. Stir in the celery with garlic and cook them for 6 min.

- Lay half of the noodles in the bottom of the casserole dish. Drain half of the beef mix and spread it over it.

- Lay on top half of the tomato followed by half of the soup and half of the cheese. Repeat the process to the remaining ingredients to make another layer of them.

- Place the casserole in the oven and let it cook for 1 h. Serve it hot.

- Get a large mixing bowl:

- Enjoy.

SERVINGS: 4

Preparation 25 mins

NUTRITIONAL INFORMATION:

Calories 737.5, Fat 29.9g, Cholesterol 169.7mg, Sodium 894.6mg, Carbohydrates 76.5g, Protein 39.7g

HOMEMADE AMISH NOODLES

INGREDIENTS

- 2 1/2 C. all-purpose **flour**

- 1 tsp **salt**

- 2 **eggs**, beaten

- 1/2 C. **milk**

- 2 tbsp **butter**, melted

- 1 drop yellow food **coloring**

DIRECTIONS

- Get a large mixing bowl: Combine in it the flour with salt. Mix in it the egg with milk, butter and food coloring.

- Knead the dough with your hands or a stand mixer for 6 min until it becomes soft. Cover it with a kitchen towel and let it rest for 12 min.

- Transfer the dough to a lightly floured surface. Use a rolling to flatten the dough until it becomes 1/4 inch thick.

- Slice into long strips and place them aside to rest for a few minutes.

- Bring a large salted pot of water to a boil. Cook in it the pasta until it become soft then serve it.

- Enjoy.

SERVINGS: 4

Preparation

- Total Time

NUTRITIONAL INFORMATION:

Calories 390.5, Fat 10.0g, Cholesterol 112.5mg, Sodium 684.0mg, Carbohydrates 61.2g , Protein 12.2g

WHIPPED LEMON TART

INGREDIENTS

- 3 oz. lemon **pudding mix**

- 1 oz. Knox unflavored **gelatin**

- 1 C. granulated **sugar**

- 2 1/4 C. **water**

- 2 tbsp **lemon** juice

- 3 **egg** yolks

- 1 tsp grated **lemon** rind

- 1 tbsp **butter**, melted

- 3 **egg** whites

- 1 C. **Cool Whip**

- 1 9-inch baked **pie crust**

DIRECTIONS

- Place a heavy saucepan over medium heat: Stir in it pudding mix, gelatin, sugar, 1/4 C. water and lemon juice.

- Mix in the egg yolks with the rest of the water. Heat them through while stirring all the time. Stir in the butter with lemon rind and turn off the heat to make the filling.

- Get a large mixing bowl: Cream in it the egg whites until their soft peaks.

- Pour the filling into a mixing bowl after it cools down for a while.

- Fold into it the egg white.

- Pour the filling into the pie shell and place it in the in the fridge to sit for 1 h.

- Once the time is up, cream the cool whip and use a piping bag to garnish the pie with it. Place it back in the fridge until ready to serve.

- Enjoy.

SERVINGS: 8

Preparation 15 mins- -**Total Time** 20 mins

NUTRITIONAL INFORMATION:

Calories 336.0, Fat 13.2g, Cholesterol 74.6mg, Sodium 308.7mg, Carbohydrates 48.7g, Protein 6.8g

CRISCO AND BUTTERMILK COOKIES

INGREDIENTS

- 2 C. **sugar**

- 1 C. **Crisco**

- 4 large **eggs**

- 4 tsp **vanilla** extract

- 4 C. **flour**

- 4 tsp **baking powder**

- 2 tsp **baking soda**

- 1 tsp **salt**

- 1 C. **buttermilk**

DIRECTIONS

- Before you do anything, preheat the oven to 425 F. Line up a baking sheet and place it aside.

- Get a large mixing bowl: Beat in it the sugar and Crisco until they become light. Mix in the eggs gradually.

- Fold the vanilla into the mix and place it aside.

- Get another mixing bowl: Stir in it the flour, baking powder, baking soda and salt. Fold it in the eggs batter with buttermilk gradually.

- Use a round spoon to drop mounds of dough in the cookie sheet.

- Place it in the oven and let them cook for 7 min.

- Place the cookies aside to lose heat completely then serve them.

- Enjoy.

SERVINGS: 1

Preparation 15 mins- -**Total Time** 25 mins

NUTRITIONAL INFORMATION:

Calories 938.3, Fat 38.6g, Cholesterol 142.6mg, Sodium 1140.6mg, Carbohydrates 133.5g , Protein 14.1g

TARTAR TART

INGREDIENTS

- 1 C. white **sugar**

- 2 tbsp **flour**

- 1 **egg**, beaten

- 1 C. **molasses**

- 2 C. **water**

- 1 tsp **vanilla**

- 2 C. **flour**

- 1 C. **brown sugar**

- 1 tsp **baking soda**

- 1 tsp cream of **tartar**

- 1/4 C. **butter**

- 1/4 C. **shortening**

2 9-INCH PIE SHELLS, UNBAKED

DIRECTIONS

- Before you do anything, preheat the oven to 350 F.

- Place a heavy saucepan over medium heat: Stir in it the white sugar, 4 Tbsp flour, egg, molasses, water, and vanilla.

- Cook them until it starts boiling. Turn off the heat and place the mix aside to lose heat for a while to make the filling.

- Get a large mixing bowl: Stir in it 2 C. flour, brown sugar, baking soda, cream of tartar, butter, and shortening. Mix them well until you get a crumbly mix.

- Divide the filling between the 2 pie shells. Sprinkle the crumble mix over them. Place the tarts in the oven and let them cook for 44 to 46 min.

- Place the aside to cool down completely. Place the tarts in the fridge until ready to serve.

- Enjoy.

SERVINGS: 1

Preparation 20 mins- -**Total Time** 1 hr

NUTRITIONAL INFORMATION:

Calories 3198.7, Fat 114.8g, Cholesterol 166.7mg, Sodium 1916.9mg, Carbohydrates 521.2g, Protein 28.6g

FLUFF COOKIES

INGREDIENTS

- 2 large **egg** yolks

- 1 1/2 C. **sugar**

- 2/3 C. **milk**

- 1 (1 oz.) package unflavored **gelatin** 1/2 C. cold **water**

- 2 **egg** whites

- 1 C. **cream**, whipped

- 3 tbsp **butter**

- 3 tbsp brown **sugar**, packed

- 12 graham **crackers**

DIRECTIONS

- Place a heavy saucepan over medium heat: Whisk in it the milk with sugar and egg yolks. Let the mixture cook until it becomes slightly thick.

- Get a small mixing bowl: Stir in the cold water with gelatin. Mix it into the hot mixture. Place the aside to cool down until it become thick.

- Get a large mixing bowl: Beat in it the egg whites until their soft peaks.

- Get another mixing bowl: Beat in it the cream until it soft peaks.

- Fold the egg white with cream into the egg yolk mixture after it cools down.

- Get a large mixing bowl: Combine in it the butter, brown sugar and crackers well.

- Spread half of the mix in the bottom of a lined up casserole dish.

- Spread over the cream then sprinkle the remaining crumbs mix on top.

- Place the casserole in the fridge for at least 4 or an overnight.

- Slice it into squares then serve it.

- Enjoy.

SERVINGS: 12

Preparation 20 mins- -**Total Time** 25 mins

NUTRITIONAL INFORMATION:

Calories 251.5, Fat 11.0g, Cholesterol 62.3mg, Sodium 88.7mg, Carbohydrates 35.1g, Protein 4.4g

NUTTY BROWNIES

INGREDIENTS

- 4 oz. baking chocolate squares

- 1 C. butter, softened

- 2 C. sugar

- 4 large eggs, beaten

- 2 tbsp vanilla

- 1 dash salt

- 1 C. flour

- 2 C. chopped nuts

DIRECTIONS

- Before you do anything, preheat the oven to 350 F. Grease a baking pan and place it aside.

- Place a heavy saucepan over medium heat. Stir in it the butter with chocolate until they melt.

- Turn off the heat. Mix into them the rest of the ingredients. Pour the mixture into the pan.

- Place it in the oven and let it cook for 22 min. Allow it to cool down completely then slice it into squares and serve it.

- Enjoy.

SERVINGS: 24

Preparation 10 mins- -**Total Time** 30 mins

NUTRITIONAL INFORMATION:

Calories 341.8, Fat 25.6g, Cholesterol 51.3mg, Sodium 167.7mg, Carbohydrates 30.1g, Protein 6.4g

RITZ CHICKEN BAKE

INGREDIENTS

- 1 loaf pan cornbread, crumbled (8x8-inch) 6 slices bread, crumbled

- 1/4 lb Ritz crackers or 1/4 lb saltine crackers, crumbled 1/2 C. butter or 1/2 C. margarine

- 1 C. coarsely chopped onion

- 1 C. coarsely chopped celery

- 2 tsp bell seasoning (or other chicken seasoning with a thyme and sage type mixture)

- salt and pepper, to taste

- 4 1/2 C. chicken broth (or broth made from a whole chicken, approximate measure, see recipe)

- 4 eggs, beaten

- 1/2 C. milk

- 1/2 tsp baking powder

- 3 -4 C. diced cooked chicken (or the meat from one whole chicken, about 4 to 4 1/2 lbs, cooked with water and seasonings to make)

- 3/4 C. dried cranberries (optional) Directions

- Place a large pot of water over high heat and bring it to a boil.

- Place in it the chicken and let it cook for 1 h with your favorite seasoning.

- Drain the chicken and reserve the broth. Remove the meat from the bones and cut it into bite size pieces.

- Before you do anything, preheat the oven to 425 F.

- Get a large mixing bowl: Stir in it the cornbread, bread, and crackers. Place it aside.

- Place a large pan over medium heat. Heat the butter in until it melts. Sauté in it the celery with onion for 5 min.

- Add them to the cornbread mix with bell seasoning, a pinch of salt and pepper. Drizzle over them some broth to and mix them until they become slightly moist.

- Mix in it the eggs with milk into them. Add enough broth until you get a slushy mix.

- Stir in the diced chicken. Pour the mix into a greased casserole dish. Place it in the oven and let it cook for 20 to 30 min. Serve it warm.

- Enjoy.

SERVINGS: 8

Preparation 25 mins

NUTRITIONAL INFORMATION:

Calories 387.4, Fat 22.7g, Cholesterol 177.7mg, Sodium 863.9mg, Carbohydrates 22.4g, Protein 22.3g